The Smart Kid's Survival Guide

Making Good Choices in a Confusing World

Patricia A. Farrell, Ph.D.

ISBN: 979-8-9986832-9-9

Books by Patricia A. Farrell, Ph.D.

When You Can't Pour From an Empty Glass: CBT Skills for Exhausted Caregivers

The Little Book on Learning Big Critical Thinking Skills

How to Be Your Own Therapist

It's Not All in Your Head: Anxiety, Depression, Mood Swings and Multiple Sclerosis

Unfiltered: Beneath the noise of our thoughts lies the true narrative of our minds

Unfiltered Again: A behind-the-scenes look at healthcare, medicine and mental health

A Social Security Disability Psychological Claims Handbook: A simple guide to understanding your SSD claim for psychological impairments and unraveling the maze of decision-making

A Social Security Disability Psychological Claims Guidebook for Children's Benefits

The Disability Accessible US Parks in All 50 States: A Comprehensive Guide

Birding in the US NOW!: A birding guide for individuals with disabilities

PATRICIA A. FARRELL, PH.D.

Contents

Introduction

Welcome to Your Amazing Thinking Adventure!

Have you ever wondered why some kids seem to figure things out so quickly? Or why sometimes you feel confused when there's too much going on around you? Well, guess what? The thinking machine you own is the best in existence, and it sits in the middle of your head.

What Makes This Book Special?

This isn't just any ordinary book. The book leads readers to become **Thinking Detectives** who solve problems and choose wisely and assist their loved ones in unexpected ways.

Inside these pages, you'll meet kids just like you:

- Maya, who discovered she has two thinking helpers in her brain
- Jake, who learned the truth about his "lucky" socks
- Emma, who figured out how to handle too many choices
- Sam, who became a real-life **truth detective**
- And many more friends who will show you their thinking secrets!

What You'll Learn to Do

When you complete this journey, you will:

- Learn how your brain operates as an amazing tool yet sometimes creates misleading situations that are amusing.

- Learn to be a fact-checking detective who can identify true facts from false information

- Learn to make better decisions, regardless of whether there is adult supervision.

- Explain your ideas clearly—so everyone understands your brilliant thoughts

- Work with smart computers—and know when to trust them and when to think for yourself

- Stay calm when things get stressful—because *a relaxed brain thinks better than a worried one*

The Best Part? You don't have to do this alone!

I made this book for you and your parent, grandparent, guardian, loving relative, or teacher to read together. The information both of you gain will be fascinating. This book lets you *form thinking partnerships* with others through its activities and thinking games. I'll bet you never thought of things that way, did you? Well, that's part of this wonderful journey.

Are you prepared to begin your adventure?

Every chapter has:

- A fun story about kids who face the same challenges you do
- Simple activities that feel more like games than homework
- Cool illustrations that bring the ideas to life
- Real-life examples you can use with friends, at school, and at home

Remember: These skills are for you growing up. No, your present thinking method doesn't need correction; it needs a bit of tuning up. Your brain already shows amazing abilities, and these tools will sharpen your use of them.

And before we begin, let's *answer one simple question*: When we say "critical," *do we always mean negative*? No, when we say "critical," we indicate that we are thinking about the information and intelligently questioning where it came from, what it means, who believes it, and what is fact and what is fiction. Critical thinking is a very important skill for all of us to have.

Think of this book as a video game guide—except instead of helping you beat levels in a game, it's helping you in real life. Your skills will improve with practice, as they do in most of the games you love to play. Did you quickly learn to play video games or outdoor games? It's the same here. You'll learn something, build on it, and become better at it in the end. It's all a matter of *adding skill to skill to skill*. Kind of like catching a ball, playing tennis, or even bike riding. Do you remember your concern about riding a bike for the first time? You had to have Mom or Dad hold the seat while they walked next to you. Then they let go, and you found out that you could ride a bike by yourself. It was wonderful! You're going to learn something wonderful here, too.

Choose a comfortable place together with your reading companion to start your outstanding adventure. **Your thinking adventure starts... right now!**

Parent Note: This book is to be read together, fostering conversation and shared learning. You'll find that some of the text shows family activity suggestions and discussion prompts.

Chapter 1: Your Amazing Thinking Brain

Each day, Samantha asked lots of questions of the people around her. "*Why is the sky blue*?" Then she wondered whether birds possess an unknown something that guides their flight routes when they migrate. She wanted to ask her mother why triangle-cut sandwiches tasted better than regular ones, but her mother didn't know the answer.

A wonderful world of questioning came into her mind every day, and in some ways it was a delight, but in others she felt let down without a perfect answer. Why didn't people know? What was the problem? How come there were no answers? So much to know and yet so little that anybody could offer in response to her questions.

During her walk to school, Samantha found herself lost in math thoughts until a red ball suddenly was headed straight for her. Quickly, Samantha jumped to the side without giving her brain any warning. The ball missed her as it flew to the other side before hitting the street.

"Nice move!" Ben arrived behind her while calling out his praise. *"How did you react so fast?"*

Samantha stopped walking. *"You know what? I have no idea. The action happened automatically and I didn't think. I just... moved."*

Ben continued to look at her as he adjusted his backpack. *"You know,"* he said, *"every math problem always means intense concentration from me while I do my homework sessions. Your reaction time was really something, and your thinking ability was in an instant."*

Samantha tilted her head, curious. *"Maybe our brains work differently for different things?"*

The next afternoon, Samantha began a detective investigation to uncover the secrets of her own thinking.

The Great Brain Investigation

Samantha took a seat at her kitchen table while using her favorite purple pen alongside a notebook. Her first note on the page read, "How Does My Brain Work?"

She began her analysis with the morning incident of the ball. What had happened? Thinking, she wrote, "I moved without thinking." The situation made no sense. The movement required mental thought, so I should have thought about it... didn't I?

Samantha recalled sitting in her math class that day as she worked on word problems. During class, Mrs. Rodriguez asked students to solve this problem about Sarah's sticker distribution: *"Sarah gives eight stickers to friends from her 24-sticker collection. What number of stickers does Sarah keep?"*

The process required Samantha to read the problem twice before creating mental images of Sarah with her stickers and performing the subtraction of 8 from 24. She needed almost two full minutes to ensure her solution was correct.

The time required for math problems extends forever, according to Samantha's written notebook. Next, she wrote "But dodging the ball was instant" in her notebook. Dodging the ball took no time at all."

Dr. Morgan served as a teacher who enjoyed teaching students about learning processes, and she was also Samantha's mother. When Samantha started writing rapidly in her notebook, Dr. Morgan took a seat beside her after returning from work.

"Mom, I think I have two different brains," Samantha announced seriously.

Dr. Morgan smiled. *"Tell me more about that."*

During the morning, Samantha had leaped away from a ball before realizing what she had done. But in math class, she had to think really hard about every step. The two thinking modes operate at different speeds because they function like fast and slow systems, she thought.

The sudden excitement in Dr. Morgan's eyes became visible. The concept that Samantha discovered has fascinated scientists for many years. Her observation about thinking functions was correct because we do possess two approaches to things, according to a theory.

The Two Thinking Helpers

Now she drew a large circle on the paper. The big circle on the paper was labeled by Dr. Morgan as "brain." *"Your brain contains two exceptional thinking assistants, which function within its structure."*

She illustrated a tiny cartoon figure with energetic traits on the left side of the circular representation. The cartoon character featured lightning bolts surrounding its body as it positioned itself to start a racing competition.

Dr. Morgan introduced the Fast-Thinking Helper as the brain part that functions quickly. This helper is speedy. The helper aids us to perform three fundamental tasks, which include *ball catching, face recognition, and basic arithmetic operations* without manual counting.

The girl agreed. She used the tool that worked for her ball escape.

"Exactly!" Dr. Morgan wrote the following character on the right-hand side of the circle. This character in the drawing showed deep thinking while wearing small glasses and holding a mini notebook.

This was her Slow-Thinking Helper. The helper operates with patience while proceeding with deliberate steps. Your Slow-Thinking Helper enables word-problem solving together with decision-making about weather clothing choices and emotional understanding for friends.

The drawing caught Samantha's attention. *"So the Fast Helper is like... automatic?"*

"The method you explained is wonderful," according to her mother. "Your Fast-Thinking Helper has learned through practice so many things that it performs them automatically without your awareness. Every time you see a dog, your brain instantly recognizes it without requiring the thinking process of "four legs, fur, tail, barks."

And the Slow Helper?

The Slow-Thinking Helper becomes active during tasks that require full concentration. The process of learning something new and ensuring correct results requires the use of this thinking approach.

Samantha was fascinated. *"Do both helpers work at the same time?"*

Dr. Morgan explained that the two helpers work together occasionally. *"But usually, one takes the lead depending on what you're doing. The trick is learning when to trust your Fast Helper and when to slow down and let your Slow Helper take charge."*

Samantha's Thinking Helper Experiments

Samantha developed into a thinking detective in the following days. She kept her purple notebook by her side at all times to record Fast and Slow-Thinking Helper activities.

Fast Helper Discoveries:

- She realized her best friend Zoe's sadness through facial expression alone.

- She successfully trapped the lunch tray as it began to slide away from her hands.

- She sang her favorite song without thinking about the words.

- She recognized that her quiet little brother was planning something mischievous.

Slow Helper Discoveries:

- She chose which book to borrow from the library.

- She organized items for her trip to spend the night at Grandma's house.

- She worked on the step-by-step process of her plant science research project.

- She needed to identify why school talent show nervousness was affecting her.

The observations showed that her Fast-Thinking Helper performed well in tasks where she practiced beforehand but sometimes drew premature conclusions. This was a problem.

One lunchtime, Samantha noticed her classmate Alex sitting by himself while staring at his sandwich. Her Fast-Thinking Helper immediately decided, "*Alex is sad.*"

Samantha recalled what her mother said regarding her two thinking helpers. She made a decision to use her Slow-Thinking Helper.

"*Wait,*" Samantha thought. "*Alex might be sad. He seemed preoccupied with eating his sandwich. He could be thinking about something fascinating at that moment. Or maybe he's feeling sick.*"

Samantha approached Alex where he sat. "*Hey, how are you doing?*"

Alex looked up and smiled. "*Oh, hi, Samantha! I'm good. I focused on memorizing the musical words we study in our music class. Want to sit with me?*"

Samantha took her seat with a cheerful expression on her face. Her Fast-Thinking Helper provided an initial assessment, yet her Slow-Thinking Helper verified it before she made any decisions.

When Fast Thinking Gets Tricky

Over the next few days, Samantha found that her Fast-Thinking Helper was great, but occasionally gave wrong information.

The family members visited the grocery store cereal section together. She saw a cereal box with a cartoon figure, which immediately captured her attention.

"*Can we get this one?*" Samantha asked, pointing to the colorful box.

Her dad asked, "*What makes you want that cereal?*"

Samantha paused. Her Fast-Thinking Helper had made the selection before she saw what type of cereal it was. She immediately wanted the cereal because of its bright colors and fun character.

Samantha examined the box more carefully before speaking. "*Um,*" Samantha said, looking more carefully at the box. "*Actually, I'm not sure. The Fast Helper selected this cereal based on its appearance.*"

Her dad smiled. The manufacturers of cereal products intend for their box designs to activate your Fast-Thinking Helper.

Samantha read the name of the cereal and the ingredients. The product turned out to be a flavor she disliked and contained too much sugar.

"*I want to let my Slow Helper make the decision this time,*" Samantha said.

She spent time reviewing multiple cereals while checking their flavors before selecting ones she really enjoyed eating. She decided on a different cereal, which lacked cartoon characters but featured a taste she knew she enjoyed.

"*Good thinking,*" her dad said. Yes, he knew that the Fast Helper was best in many situations, yet crucial decisions needed verification from the Slow Helper.

The Thinking Helper Balance

After bed preparation, Samantha discovered another important thing about her thinking helpers.

During her tooth-brushing routine, Samantha relied on her Fast-Thinking Helper due to her years of practice, yet her mind drifted to her upcoming book report. Her Slow-Thinking Helper was currently working on deciding her book report content.

She called "*Mom*" while brushing her teeth in the bathroom. "*Can both thinking helpers work at the same time?*"

Dr. Morgan appeared in the doorway. "*What do you think?*"

She was simultaneously brushing her teeth with no conscious thought. "*My mind was focused on the upcoming book report, so I think they can both work, but on different things.*"

Her mom praised her observation skills. The familiar tasks that your Fast Helper handles simultaneously with the complex problems the Slow Helper works on. When you need to dedicate all your attention to something, it's best to focus on an activity.

Samantha nodded while she finished brushing her teeth. "*Like when I'm learning to ride my bike without training wheels. I need my Slow Helper to handle the bike's steering and balancing.*"

"Exactly. Your Fast-Thinking Helper will take care of the basic riding skills when you can ride your bike well, but your Slow Helper will handle route planning."

The Amazing Thing About Practice

Samantha thought about the transition of tasks from her Slow-Thinking Helper to her Fast-Thinking Helper while she repeated them throughout the following week.

When Samantha first began tying her shoes, she needed to focus on each step of the process: create a loop and then wrap the other lace around before pulling it through and tightening it. The process of shoe-tying required her Slow-Thinking Helper to put in significant effort.

At this point now, Samantha was able to tie her shoes without losing focus on her desired recess activity. Shoe-tying had become a Fast Helper skill.

Many tasks shifted from her Slow-Thinking Helper to her Fast-Thinking Helper during the past week.

- The process of word-by-word pronunciation used to be necessary for reading until her Fast Helper learned to instantly recognize words.

- She had to put all her attention into scooter riding but she now rides and chats with friends at the same time.

- After months of regular bed-making practice, the task became an automatic Fast Helper skill for her.

- Her Fast Helper continues to learn new abilities, which she noted in her notebook.

Samantha Becomes a Thinking Helper Teacher

At the end of the week, Samantha became so enthusiastic about her discovery that she wanted to show it to her five-year-old brother, Jake.

Samantha took a seat on the floor with her brother to give him the message. *"Did you know you have two thinking helpers in your brain?"*

Jake looked skeptical. *"I only have one brain."*

It was time to help him learn. *"Your brain is one piece, but it operates through two different mental ways. Want me to show you?"*

- Samantha brought a ball in front of her face. I" will throw this ball toward you, so please be ready."

- Jake caught the ball effortlessly because she tossed it to him with a gentle motion.

"You knew the ball would need you to extend your hand to catch, it, but why did you do that?" Samantha asked.

Jake shrugged. *"I just did."*

"That's known as your Fast-Thinking Helper. Your fast thinking got you to catch the ball instantly before you even had to think about it."

She got a basic puzzle that had large pieces. *"Now, try to put this puzzle together."*

- During the task, Jake took his time to study the pieces carefully as he thought about the best fit for each component.

- Samantha watched his evaluation of every puzzle piece. "That's your Slow-Thinking Helper!" He was surprised.

Jake's eyes widened. *"I have two thinking helpers!"*

Throughout the rest of the afternoon, Jake identified the Fast Helper moments as he walked and spoke while recognizing his toys, and he identified his Slow Helper experiences when selecting toys and building a block tower.

The Big Lesson

During dinner, the Morgan family had a discussion about the learning experiences of Samantha from her week of doing detective work.

The decision to share her thoughts with others required careful consideration from Samantha during that evening. Her Slow-Thinking Helper naturally became active.

"I understand both types of helpers are needed because my Fast Helper works well for familiar tasks, yet my Slow Helper helps with both new things and important choices. The Slow Helper is great for things involving new experiences along with difficult choices and preventing errors."

"That's wonderful," her dad said. *"What else?"*

Thoughtfully, she said, *"My Fast Helper makes fast decisions through its impulsive, quick nature, especially when exciting situations happen. I need to use my Slow Helper whenever I make important choices."*

Jake piped up. *"And I learned that when I practice something a lot, it moves from my Slow Helper to my Fast Helper!"* They'd both learned something new.

Samantha smiled at Jake as she stood up beside him. *"Exactly!"*

Dr. Morgan smiled at both of her children. Both of them had discovered an essential truth that will assist them throughout their entire lives. People who think effectively understand which times to depend on their Fast Helper and which times need a more thoughtful approach.

NOTE: The subject of this section is cognition, a term that may not be familiar to your child and needs to be explained so that they can understand it. What is cognition? Here's a quick explanation:

Cognition refers to **thinking activities** that describe how your brain *operates to learn and solve problems*. Your brain uses cognition to remember toy locations and solve puzzles and learn new school material. The brain performs all its intelligent operations through cognition to help you understand your environment.

Activities for Young Thinking Detectives

Activity 1: The Thinking Helper Diary

Create a basic notebook for one day to document examples of your use of both thinking helpers. Drawing pictures should accompany the writing.

Fast Helper Examples Might Include:

- The ability to catch objects that fall to the ground

- The ability to recognize a friend who stands at a distance

- Your body automatically uses the appropriate writing hand

- You easily remember to sing a familiar song

Slow Helper Examples Might Include:

- Choosing clothing based on weather conditions

- Learning the rules of a new game

- Creating a plan for telephone calls to Grandma

- Doing homework

Activity 2: The Speed Test Game

Try these simple tasks and notice which thinking helper you use:

Quick Questions (Fast Helper):

- What's 2 + 2?

- What color is grass?

- What sound does a dog make?

Thinking Questions (Slow Helper):
- If you have 3 boxes and each box has 4 toys, how many toys do you have in total?

- How would the world change if water droplets started rising towards the sky instead of falling down?

- What would be the way to describe the color blue to someone who has never experienced colors before?

Activity 3: The Practice Investigation

Select an area you are currently learning about (biking, musical instruments, or new games). Each day, notice:
- Does it feel easier than yesterday?

- Can you perform it with other thoughts distracting you?

- Are there parts that still require your Slow Helper?

- Observe the way skills progress from requiring *Slow Helper to becoming Fast Helper*.

Activity 4: The Decision Detective Game

The next time you face a decision about what to put on, which book to read, or what activity to engage in, use the following process:
- Your Fast Helper immediately wants to select what option at this point.

- Your Slow Helper requires you to pose which questions?

- Are the choices identical or distinct from each other?

- What advice from either helper is most suitable for this situation?

Questions for Family Discussion

1. Can you recall an instance where your Fast-Thinking Helper assisted you? What about your Slow-Thinking Helper?

2. Are there specific occasions that require you to trust your Fast Helper? When is it better to use your Slow Helper?

3. You have moved from needing your Slow Helper to complete this action, which you now accomplish with your Fast Helper.

4. How does understanding your two thinking helpers enable better performance at school? At home? With friends?

5. How would you advise a friend who rushes into decisions? How about a friend who delays every decision?

A Note for Parents and Caregivers

This chapter presented an appropriate version for children about dual-process thinking. The cognitive science describes this dual thinking process as **System 1** (fast automatic intuitive) and **System 2** (slow deliberate analytical) based on the work of psychologist **Dr. Daniel Kahneman**.

The knowledge of these two thinking systems enables children to:

- Build metacognitive skills that help them monitor their thinking process

- Acquire skills to recognize when to rely on quick instincts or when to pause for evaluation

- Better understand their learning process

- The ability to be patient when dealing with activities that need thorough consideration

Your child should learn to:
- Observe their mental operations between quick and slow thinking

- Learn to transition between fast and slow thinking at the right times

- Both types of thinking bring important value to the table

- The development of skills results in their transition from slow to fast mental processing

The goal is not to use slow thinking at all times but to learn when to select the appropriate thinking approach.

The thinking helper's journey of Samantha has only started. She will discover in the following chapter how to handle information with care since our Fast-Thinking Helper may believe untrue things sometimes.

The entire chapter focuses on encouraging your children to ask questions. It brings to mind something I experienced while consulting at a company. A woman walked up to me and wanted to ask about an interaction between her son and her husband the previous evening. The boy had come home and asked his parents a question about sex. Immediately, the father smacked the boy in the face and said, *"Don't ever ask about that again!"*

This is an illustration of how important children's questions that should be brought into the home for guidance from the parents have been shut off. After this interaction, the boy will know it's not safe to question his parents. Will it be safe to question anything or only certain subjects? Now, he will question on the street, and what kinds of answers will he receive?

Chapter 2: The Case of Jake's Lucky Socks

Jake Martinez was convinced that his red lightning bolt socks were the secret to winning soccer matches. Each time his team won a game, he wore bright red socks with yellow lightning bolts on them. *"These socks bring me good luck,"* Jake shouted to his teammates after their third win of the season. *Yes, he knew, and no one else could convince him that it wasn't so.*

Are you sure that Jake socks brought him and his teammates all those wins? His friend Maya wasn't so sure, and you could tell by the way she was raising one eyebrow and looking at him. *"How do you know it's really the socks?"*

The answer was simple for Jake. *"Easy! Our victories occur every time I use them. We lost the game last week because I forgot my socks. The socks are magic!"*

Maya showed an interest in understanding the theory Jake had about his lucky socks. But she learned about **confirmation bias** during her science class, which describes how people notice only supporting evidence for their beliefs while refusing to see contradictory evidence. It was pretty clear to Maya, but not to Jake.

The suggestion from Maya was to *work as detectives*. She began to ask him if he remembered the outcome of each match throughout the current season.

Jake retrieved his soccer journal with all the game records from their season. Then they created an *organized table* for checking the scores.

Games with Red Lightning Socks:

- On September 5th, the team won a 3-2 victory

- On September 12th, our team got a 1-0 victory

- The team then went on to a 2-1 victory on September 19th

- The game on October 3 ended in a 0-1 loss

- The team had two losses on October 10th when the score ended 2-3

Games with Regular Socks:

- The team managed a 4-1 victory on August 29th

- The match on September 26 resulted in a loss with a 2-1 score

- Our team again had a 1-0 victory on October 17

The chart in front of Jake made him stare in surprise. "*Wait... Two of my 'lucky' socks matches ended in losses, while our team won games without them?*" Jake was surprised to see that the team had victories in games when he didn't wear his socks. How did that happen? Why weren't his lucky socks working?

"*Exactly*!" Maya said. "*Your belief that you were wearing red socks for success triggered your mind to look at every game where your team won. The pattern remained constant because you failed to look at all the games.*" Yes, even when he didn't wear his lucky socks, the team won games. But he didn't see that because *he was concentrating on his socks being the important factor.* And he only looked at winning games when he was wearing the socks.

Scientists call this behavior "**confirmation bias**" because we focus on *evidence that supports our existing beliefs* while ignoring any evidence that doesn't support our beliefs. What keeps us from looking at evidence that doesn't fit with our beliefs?

Why Our Brains Do This

Our brains function like high-speed computers with built-in operational shortcuts, which sometimes create misleading results. Yes, our brains use biases to speed up decision-making processes while leading us to overlook **important details.**

Confirmation bias happens because:

1. *Pattern-seeking*: Our brains **love finding patterns**, even when they don't really exist

2. *Selective attention*: We **notice things that fit** our expectations quicker. In life this is also called "*The Cocktail Party Effect*" where we selectively attend to people and conversations.

3. *Memory bias*: We **remember successes** more clearly than failures. Failure isn't something we'd rather forget.

4. *Comfort zone*: It **feels good** when our beliefs are confirmed. Don't we enjoy being right?

Becoming a Truth Detective

Through her investigation of Jake's lucky sock theory, Maya showed how we can become better truth detectives by **asking important questions.**

The Detective's Toolkit:

Question 1: "*What evidence do I have?*" Examine all existing evidence instead of focusing only on times things seemed to work correctly.

Question 2: "*Am I only noticing what I want to see?*" Make an effort to find examples that oppose your belief.

Question 3: "*Could there be another explanation?*" The team achieved victory because they dedicated more practice time and enjoyed better weather conditions while facing inferior opponents. That's certainly possible and would rule out the lucky socks idea. Always look for alternative reasons why something might have happened.

Question 4: "*What would prove me wrong?*" A good detective must *always think about the evidence* that would shift their view.

Facts vs. Opinions: Learning the Difference

A critical thinker must *distinguish between facts and opinions* because this understanding builds their thinking abilities.

Facts are statements that *can be proven true or false* with evidence like:

- The soccer ball is a round object.

- Our team scored two goals.

- The rain fell during the previous day's game. So, the weather played a role.

Opinions are personal beliefs, feelings, or judgments like:

- Soccer stands as the best sport in the world, according to my view.

- I consider red to be my lucky color.

- Our coach is really nice.

People often present their opinions as if they were facts, which creates confusion. Knowing how to distinguish between facts and opinions helps us to develop better critical thinking skills.

Practice Activity: Fact or Opinion Detective

Examine these statements to determine if they belong to the "Fact" or "Opinion" category.

1. *"Chocolate ice cream tastes better than vanilla."*
2. *"There are 24 hours in a day."*
3. *"Everyone should exercise until they're exhausted every day."*
4. *"Water boils at 100 degrees Celsius (212 degrees Fahrenheit)."*
5. *"That movie was boring."*
6. *"The library has 500 books."*
7. *"Pizza is the perfect food."*
8. *"Plants need sunlight to grow."*

Answers: *Facts*: 2, 4, 6, 8 | *Opinions*: 1, 3, 5, 7

What Jake Learned

Jake discovered that his soccer success depended more on his team's *training and strategy and teamwork* than on his choice of socks.

He admitted to Maya that he had become so enthusiastic about discovering a "magic" solution that he focused on times when it seemed to work.

Maya smiled and offered an answer. *"That's totally normal! Our brains do that to everyone. The important thing is that when we realize it's happening, we can become better thinkers."*

Now Jake kept his red lightning bolt socks *because he enjoyed them* rather than believing in their supposed luck.

His soccer performance increased a great deal after he *stopped depending on superstition* and focused on developing his athletic abilities through practice.

Chapter Summary

Key Lessons:

- We notice evidence that supports our beliefs yet disregard evidence that contradicts them because of confirmation bias.

- The task of a "truth detective" requires us to examine the total evidence rather than selecting favorable parts.

- Evidence can prove facts, while personal beliefs represent opinions.

- Our brains operate naturally with these mental shortcuts, but understanding them helps us develop better thinking abilities.

- The best way for us to evaluate our beliefs requires actively searching for evidence that challenges our current perspective.

- Good critical thinkers should question their own beliefs at the same level as they question claims made by others. By staying curious and open-minded, we can discover what's really true instead of just what we want to believe.

Chapter 3:
Too Much
Information!

The love of reading books ranked as Emma Chen's favorite pastime, ahead of every other activity. Emma's heart filled with excitement after her teacher told them students could pick any book for their reading project, which lasted one month. This was going to be the best assignment ever! She just knew it.

The following day after her classes, Emma rushed to the town library with her mother. She had entered this library countless times before, yet the current visit felt different. Today, she needed to select the ideal book for her assignment. When Emma entered the library, she immediately became overwhelmed because of the many choices surrounding her. How could she choose? It was almost too much for her to consider, and something wonderful was turning into a difficulty. Why?

The children's section contained thousands of books that filled row after row of shelves. Here, the library collection included picture books and books to read that were mystery novels, science fiction adventures, and biographies about famous people, as well as guides for building robots. Emma looked at different bookshelves while her eyes scanned colorful covers and interesting titles from unknown authors. So much to choose from. It was even more than she had hoped for, but it was proving to be stressful.

The many options made Emma begin asking her mother for help while she displayed both enthusiasm and nervousness. Which book of all these choices should she pick? It was a little upsetting for Emma.

Her mom smiled knowingly. "*Having too many choices makes everything seem overwhelming to you and everyone else.*" This wasn't always what we had thought it might be.

Emma nodded vigorously. She had faced this experience many times while selecting streaming content from movie and show lists and school cafeteria food options between different stations. But, somehow, this situation seemed more critical than the previous experiences she had faced. Her class project grade would be decided based on the book she chose. But what book?

She decided to start systematically, beginning with the fantasy section since she had enjoyed reading about wizards and magical creatures in the past. Among the many books within the single fantasy category, Emma discovered an overwhelming number of books. The fantasy section at the library contained several types, including thick novels with dragon and castle artwork and short magical school series and standalone stories about children who discover hidden abilities. Multiple books displayed awards and quotes from famous authors and characters that matched her age group.

Emma selected several books from the shelves to read the back covers and first pages of each book. All the books appeared to offer their own unique level of interest. The first book presented a main character who communicated with animals, while the second introduced a hero who learned his family came from ancient kings, and the third followed twins who could move between different dream worlds. Each summary presented the book as both exciting and wonderful. But she had to choose only one book to read for the assignment. Just one book!

After an hour of searching through the shelves, Emma gathered fifteen books that appeared promising to her. She faced greater uncertainty instead of accomplishment after gathering all the books. Choosing between fifteen interesting options presented a difficult task for her since she needed to select only one. What if she picked the wrong book and missed out on something even better? She would be stuck with a dull book that she chose, which could be uninteresting, and she would have to keep reading it for the entire month. Instead of being something wonderful, it would be almost like punishment. It was almost too much for her to think about.

Emma's mom watched as her daughter became increasingly frustrated. She noticed her daughter's face showed signs of struggling with her decision. and she wanted to help.

There were so many great books available to choose from! Emma pointed to her massive book pile while saying, "*There are just too many good books!*" Emma pointed at her now towering stack with some concern. "*And that's only from the fantasy section. I haven't explored the mystery section, the science section and the graphic novels yet. I would probably discover a better book somewhere else, but I spent all my time studying these books.*"

"**Information overload**" is the term that describes the experience that Emma is currently undergoing. Our world presents us with more information and choices than any previous generation faced in human history. Many choices bring wonderful benefits, but they also create paralysis because we lack the skills to *identify what truly matters* among all available options.

In the library reading corner, Emma sat down with her mother beside her. "*Our library contained fewer books when I was your age compared to the current facility,*" she explained. "*The whole children's section contained approximately fifty books at that time. The first impression might be that few options were available, yet the selection process proved simpler than you'd expect. Every single option was accessible to me because the selection wasn't very large.*"

Emma considered this. "*If the fifty books in the library didn't capture your interest, you would have felt disappointed, wouldn't you?*"

"*That's a great question,*" her mom replied. "*Fewer options could stop us from seeking the perfect content.*" But her mother also realized there was another problem, and that it was in seeking the "perfect" content of any book.

Emma was experiencing information overload, and she recognized it. More than an hour passed at the library, yet she had not made a single book selection. The overwhelming feeling at the start had not only persisted but worsened into complete confusion. The more she looked, the worse she felt.

"*So how do I decide?*" Emma asked. All these choices seemed to make her decision process too stressful.

Her mom understood. "*There absolutely is a way to decide. The process involves skills to evaluate information and select choices that matter most to you instead of attempting to examine all available options.*"

Things were beginning to clear up as Emma and her mom created a plan to handle the overwhelming amount of information together. They began by determining *what specific goals she wanted to achieve* through her reading project. The reading project required her to decide between hard-to-read, challenging books and enjoyable simple ones. *The goal was to gain new information in some categories* or, if she preferred, to read about thrilling adventures. She preferred reading about people who were her age, but she also wanted to explore stories about adults.

Emma carefully weighed the questions that were presented. She identified her main priority as *finding a book that would keep her interested* throughout the month without becoming too challenging. But she needed to read stories with relatable characters while also wanting to experience a world that differed from her regular environment. She wanted to learn, but she wanted it to be interesting and to hold her attention.

By considering these criteria, Emma pulled out several books from her selection and set them aside. At this time, the novel about ancient gods was too complex and serious for her needs. The book about twins navigating through dreams appeared to present potentially understandable challenges for readers. The animal dialogue story fascinated her, yet its everyday setting mirrored her daily environment. No, she wanted a challenge and a change of pace in terms of life.

After filtering the books, Emma reduced her choices from fifteen to five, which became a more workable number. The following strategy involved setting a time restriction for Emma to evaluate all the remaining books. Emma read the initial page of each story while paying attention to her instant reaction instead of studying multiple pages from each book. In one of her classes on writing assignments, her teacher had indicated that the first 10 pages or even less in a book could tell you a lot about it and if you'd enjoy it.

Emma found the opening page of her first book interesting, although it didn't fully capture her interest. The writing quality was good, but the main character failed to create any connection with her.

But there was a difference with the second book. The character's bravery combined with the first page's exciting content without confusion, made it instantly appealing to her.

Instead of trying to evaluate all five remaining books, Emma decided to select the second book without hesitation. Her mom looked puzzled and asked if she would read the opening pages of the other three books before making a decision.

Emma displayed her disagreement through a firm headshake. "*I preferred this choice. I think more searching will only create confusion.*" Good-enough decisions usually yield better results than perfect choices because perfect decisions require so much time that people miss out on the enjoyment of their final selection. Is there anything such as a perfect choice?

The book selection had led Emma to learn something extremely important. Research conducted by psychologists demonstrates that too much decision-making time can lead to worse outcomes for choice satisfaction than *making decisions swiftly with reasonable standards.* Our minds notice every lost opportunity as we analyze choices too deeply, which can lead us to feelings of regret.

The book check-out process brought Emma contentment as she looked forward to beginning her reading. Emma's mother praised her approach during their library trip. "*You made an intelligent move in that moment,*" she said. She determined her priorities to reduce her options and then made a timely decision before she began to feel that she had given up something by selecting only one. Taking too much time for some choices may mean that, even if we select the thing we like most, we may feel we have lost out on something. In that case, we don't even feel happy about the choice that we made, even if it was a great choice.

Emma laughed. "*It's kind of like cleaning my room*," she said. "*I can't find things I need when everything is disorganized. I can use my stuff best when I arrange my things correctly in designated places.*" Here, Emma used an analogy.

But ***what's an analogy,*** and how can we understand them? The words *"like," "as,"* and the phrases *"similar to," "in the same way,"* and *"in a similar manner"* indicate analogies. It's a way of helping people *understand something by comparing it to something that they already know.* Here are a few examples:

- An analogy is a way to *explain unfamiliar ideas* by comparing them to something we know with new information.

- To *explain brain functions,* you would *compare it to a computer* that stores data and helps us think and remember information. Thinking is like a computer storing files and working with them.

- Your *brain* also *functions as a library* because it contains pieces of information that you can retrieve at any time.

- *Rain clouds are similar to sponges* because they absorb water until they begin releasing it.

- *Books are like doors* because they provide access to new destinations and exciting experiences.

Emma's analogy impressed her mother because of its accuracy. "*That's exactly right. Information functions similarly to physical possessions because proper organization helps, yet excessive, disorganized information leads to overwhelming situations.*" Organization, it seemed, was key to satisfaction.

After selecting her book, Emma used the lessons learned to guide her through different aspects of her life during the following weeks. Before starting her science project on ocean animals, she decided which particular ocean-related questions she needed to answer. By concentrating her research and excluding irrelevant whale migration data unrelated to coral reef studies, she could stay on course. It was working for her now in other areas of her life.

Emma decided to monitor the amount of information she gained when she had free time. After extended social media scrolling and online video watching, she experienced frequent exhaustion and mental fatigue. Her mental overload resulted from consuming too much information without any direction or filtering system.

She began calling this new habit of information selection her **"information diet"** which she decided to test. Following a food diet requires careful selection of what you consume, and an *information diet requires deliberate selection of what information you allow into your system*. Emma established particular times for social media checks instead of mindless continuous usage throughout the day. Before watching videos online, she decided her educational or entertainment goals so she could select content that matched her needs.

The results were remarkable. Through her purposeful information selection, Emma experienced *reduced anxiety levels and improved concentration*. The specific purpose she applied when approaching new information led to a better understanding and a more enjoyable learning experience.

Not only did Emma's mom notice the change, but also her teacher observed Emma experiencing this transformation. During the book report presentations, Emma confidently discussed her selected novel and effectively explained the key elements and concepts from the book. Several classmates who spent weeks switching between different books because they couldn't make up their minds appeared unprepared and unenthusiastic about their selected choices.

The situation revealed to Emma that *information filtering ability stands equal to information collection skill* because modern society presents endless data and many choices. The ability to determine your core priorities, develop clear selection guidelines, and stop searching in order to take action helps people succeed in their daily lives.

Even the lesson of "good enough" acceptance proved to be beneficial because it eliminated the need to constantly pursue perfect results. Striving for perfection prevents us from appreciating the many good options available.

During that month, Emma accomplished her book's completion and delivered exceptional presentations while developing multiple strategies for managing overwhelming choices and excessive information. The process of decision-making requires you to **ask yourself three essential questions**:

- *"What am I trying to accomplish?"*

- *"What criteria matter most to me?"*

- *"How much time should I spend on this decision?"*

Emma found that information overload and excessive choice options create normal challenges during modern life, yet there is an effective solution to manage these situations. We can learn to handle information overload and achieve our goals through the right strategies combined with appropriate mental approaches.

Your Information Diet Plan

Following Emma's example, you should develop an individual information diet plan to manage your data. The process doesn't require a complete ban on information or entertainment, but it needs you to *carefully choose what information you focus on* and *understand the purpose* behind your selections.

Track down how various sources of information affect your emotional state. Certain books and websites tend to energize your mind along with creating curiosity in you. Certain apps, when combined with specific shows, can make you feel fatigued and anxious. *Self-awareness enables you to select better ways to use your mental energy.*

Your attention represents *a valuable resource that exists in restricted quantities.* Consuming too much low-quality information is like eating junk food for every meal since it leads to mental feelings of disorganization and lack of focus. When you choose which things to focus on, you will experience greater calmness together with increased interest and purposeful daily activities.

Chapter Summary

Our experience at the library demonstrates that dealing with information-rich environments requires us to develop new methods of information selection and concentration. To handle overwhelming choices, we need to establish our priorities before making decisions. Taking a reasonably good decision quickly provides better results than prolonged searches for the perfect choice, which prevent us from experiencing what we select. Modern-world decision-making requires us to learn *information overload management skills* in order to think clearly. How we manage all the choices that are out there is very important to our happiness and our futures.

Chapter 4: Being a Truth Detective

S am Rodriguez found mysteries to be the only thing that sparked her interest. She enjoyed reading detective stories while watching mystery movies, as well as working on puzzles. The instant her brother Marcus uttered his unique statement during dinner, Sam activated her detective instincts.

"You can see in dark conditions just like a superhero if you consume enough carrots," according to Marcus as he munched his carrot stick. He said it was the explanation of why your mother requires us to eat vegetables. Sam found this unbelievable and couldn't stop herself from responding.

Her eyes widened with excitement. Having night vision abilities seemed incredibly thrilling to her. She envisioned herself performing night missions throughout the house by using perfect vision while everyone else struggled with darkness. However, she began thinking more logically. Marcus seemed believable to her, but she doubted his claim because it felt improbable.

"Really?" Sam asked skeptically. *"How do you know that's true?"*

Marcus shrugged confidently. *"Everyone knows that. Jake's father works as a physician, and Jake gets this information from school, so we can trust it."*

The answer failed to satisfy Sam's desire for information. The detective stories she loved taught her that investigators should never take anything at face value until verifying the evidence. *"I need to verify the reliability of the information about carrots and night vision because I want to be certain I won't waste my time by eating too many carrots."*

Starting the Investigation

Sam started her investigation by collecting all available data following the proper method of a detective after dinner. The first step she took was to ask her parents about their understanding regarding carrots and vision.

The beta-carotene in carrots provides eye health benefits, according to her Mom, who thoughtfully replied, *"But I'm not sure about the seeing-in-the-dark part. Where did you hear that?"*

During their conversation, Sam related Marcus's statement to her parents until she noticed them exchange a knowing smile. Her Dad chuckled. *"That's an interesting story, Sam. The information appears worthy of additional investigation. What action should a detective take next according to your assessment?"*

Sam thought about this question for a while before responding. In her preferred detective novels, she knew that investigators sought information from multiple sources before forming their opinions. And detectives avoided depending solely on statements from individuals when those statements came from secondary sources. But what are secondary sources?

An example of a secondary source is when your friend *describes a movie they saw using information they received from another source.* It wasn't something they came up with on their own. A book about dinosaurs written by scientists today serves as a secondary source because *scientists studied fossils and other evidence* to learn about dinosaurs even though they didn't exist during the scientists' lifetimes.

Sam decided to perform independent research because of her decision. *"For the information I need to trust requires verification from trustworthy sources."*

Her mom nodded approvingly. *"That's excellent thinking. What makes a source reliable should be discussed with the group."*

Understanding Source Reliability

The information from her parents showed her that *not every source delivers trustworthy information equally.* The process of detective work involves evaluating different evidence in the same way investigators evaluate their various pieces of evidence to determine their value.

Determining truth requires you to find experts who specialize in that field, according to her father. Medical information requires expertise from physicians and scientists or reputable health organizations.

The information you get from friends at school about diet differs a great deal from scientific knowledge found in books written by nutrition experts. The first impression of two different statements may appear equal, but their reliability stands at different levels.

In the process of identifying reliable sources during research, she received instruction from her mother. **Websites with edu or gov** domains provide trustworthy information better than informal social media posts and random blogs do. The quality control process for books that experts publish through reputable publishing houses includes thorough **fact-checking procedures**. News organizations with established reputations and professional journalists conduct thorough fact-checking before they publish their articles. These organizations want to publish only the best information they can glean from multiple sources to avoid harm or misunderstanding of their stories.

Reliable sources sometimes present errors, either by reporting unconfirmed research or by distributing incorrect information, according to her mother.

Good detectives always look for various reliable sources that share the same information because multiple sources help build stronger evidence, according to her Mom. A closer examination of carrot-related statements followed their discussion.

The knowledge about source reliability Sam gained led her to begin her research. She began by consulting the encyclopedia for information about carrots and vision before proceeding to search with her parents' help on established health websites.

Sam's findings were more intricate and intriguing than Marcus's basic statement. The human body changes beta-carotene from carrots into vitamin A. The human body requires vitamin A for vision functions, especially when dealing with night vision. *The process of eating carrots does not result in superhuman night vision capabilities.*

The research revealed that vitamin A deficiency leads to night blindness because people develop vision problems in low-light conditions. Carrots, along with other vitamin A-rich foods, serve as essential dietary components for people with deficiencies because they enhance dim light visibility. People who consume sufficient vitamin A through their diet won't experience any extra night vision advantages from additional carrot consumption. OK, it seems like the situation Marcus had related was not exactly correct.

Carrots enable specific individuals to see better at night, according to Sam, but they fail to provide superhero-level night vision capabilities to anyone.

Her dad smiled. "*Exactly! The way you present information affects how accurate statements become misleading to the audience.*"

The Historical Mystery

Sam encountered an intriguing new discovery during her ongoing research. She came across multiple articles that demonstrated how the belief about carrots enhancing night vision emerged from World War II propaganda efforts. What was the purpose of the propaganda, and what were its creators trying to achieve?

The British military created new radar technology, which enabled pilots to detect and destroy enemy planes in total darkness during World War II. To protect their radar technology from enemy detection, the British government *released false information* indicating that carrot consumption led to exceptional night vision capabilities among their pilots. It wasn't an accurate statement, and the military knew it, but it was intended to support their war efforts.

The propaganda efforts were so successful that many *people kept this false belief* about carrots giving night vision capabilities for multiple decades. Sam was shocked to learn that the basic health claim about carrots had a direct connection to military operations during wartime and intentional deception.

Sam felt astonishment as she told her parents about this discovery. The story about carrots exists in two parts, which *combine factual information with intentional false content used as a tool for deception.*

Her Mom nodded. "*Detectives who wish to excel in their work need to investigate thoroughly by seeking information from multiple sources. The most fascinating findings emerge from studying what people believe as well as the reasons behind their beliefs.*"

Testing the Evidence

The completion of her research depended on Sam's conducting personal tests to prove her findings. She got permission from her parents to create a basic assessment of how carrots impact human night vision abilities.

Sam ate carrots daily for two weeks while she documented any changes she observed in her ability to see during low-light conditions in her journal. She checked her ability to move through her bedroom using window light as her only source of light to detect objects.

After two weeks, Sam needed to acknowledge that her *night vision had not improved noticeably*. She continued to have the same dim-light visibility as before, and she did not develop any extraordinary night vision capabilities.

Sam concluded her research by saying that her findings supported the information she had learned. *"My healthy diet already contains enough vitamin A, so eating extra carrots made no difference."*

Her parents commended her extensive research methods for verifying the claim. She investigated dependable sources through research while conducting her experiment to validate the information firsthand.

Learning to Ask the Right Questions

The investigation about carrots taught Sam to create a set of questions, which she discovered could serve as a framework for assessing suspicious claims.

The Detective's Question Toolkit

"How do you know that?" The vital question that Sam learned to pose to others became the most crucial one in her investigative toolkit. Sam sought information about the origin of every statement made by others. Did she get the information from a trustworthy source, or did she learn it from an expert or through casually talking about unverified stories?

"*Who is the original source?*" The process of passing information between people resembles a game of telephone because details transform during each handoff. Sam developed the practice of following claims to their source whenever possible.

"*What expertise does this source have*?" Sam understood that she shouldn't consult a plumber about bicycle repairs in the same way she should not ask health questions of experts except in cases involving scientists and historians for their respective fields of study.

"*Do other reliable sources agree*?" Multiple trustworthy sources confirming the same information made the statement more likely to be accurate than a single source making the claim.

"*Could there be another explanation?*" The question enabled Sam to identify alternative explanations before drawing premature conclusions.

"*What evidence would change my mind?*" The practice of good detectives requires them to stay receptive to new evidence that may contradict their initial assumptions. Now she knew she wanted to avoid the confirmation bias she had already learned about.

Sharing the Discovery

Sam spoke to Marcus with sensitivity because she wanted to avoid causing him embarrassment from spreading false information. Good detectives dedicate their time to *uncovering facts instead of trying to prove others incorrect*, according to Sam's understanding.

Sam initiated the conversation by stating, "*I researched the information about carrots that you previously shared. My research showed that there's really interesting historical information about the topic.*"

She showed him her findings regarding vitamin A along with night blindness and the World War II propaganda effort. The historical elements of the information captured Marcus's interest, so he acknowledged that he never validated the statement when sharing it. For him, it was opening a new world of understanding. In fact, now he found he was more interested in history than he was before. This questioning had opened a new door of knowledge for him.

Marcus expressed his regret about his lack of a verification process before sharing the information with others. *"The claim appeared authentic because Jake's father practices medicine, yet I now understand that medical knowledge doesn't guarantee his accurate reports about medicine."* True, someone may be an expert in something like medicine but not in other areas.

Sam nodded. *"Medical professionals can possess incorrect knowledge outside their medical fields, and they simplify complex information when explaining to children."*

Through their discussion, Sam and Marcus learned that being an effective truth detective *requires both occasional errors and open-mindedness* to new evidence.

Daily Life Applications of Detective Methods

Sam discovered she could use her new investigative techniques in many daily encounters throughout the following weeks. Each time, her friend was asked by Sam to back her claim regarding faster running sneakers, and a joint investigation was suggested to confirm it. Sam questioned both the evidence behind the health claims of a certain snack and the definition of 'healthiest' when she saw the advertisement. Both were beginning to understand how to be information detectives.

The detective approach developed by Sam didn't result in her being doubtful or distrustful of everything she heard. The new approach helped her transform into a more analytical consumer of information. She maintained her interest in acquiring knowledge but learned how to distinguish between solidly backed information and statements that required additional verification.

Sam's ability to detect emotional manipulation in advertisements became more noticeable to her parents, who observed this change. Through her improved research skills, she located trustworthy websites, which her teachers praised during school assignments. The internet had proven more helpful than all the social media scrolling she had done on it.

The Ongoing Adventure

A truth detective must continue practicing their skills because *learning the skill once does not guarantee permanent proficiency.* Information and claims continue to appear in her life through various sources, which include social media posts and news stories and talks with her friends and family members. Her detective abilities developed with *every fresh piece of information she encountered.*

Being an effective truth detective means not having to verify every statement she encounters. That would be exhausting and unnecessary. She learned to direct her detective work at claims that hold significance or surprise value or when she needs to take action on them. There was, of course, information filtering that she had to do before she decided to expend the energy in doing the research about what she had heard.

The carrot investigation revealed to Sam that actual facts tend to be more intricate than basic statements show. The ability to detect truth in the vast information landscape became more valuable to her than acquiring superhuman night vision through carrot consumption.

The essential lesson Sam gained was that *incorrect conclusions provide valuable learning opportunities* that enhance her critical thinking abilities. Detectives who are successful at their jobs maintain their beliefs until they find superior evidence, which they welcome as evidence of mental development instead of feeling ashamed.

Becoming a Source Detective

She discovered that **knowing the source of information** is equally important as knowing the information itself. The mental tool she developed for source evaluation became a versatile method she could apply to all her information analysis needs.

When receiving new information, Sam always checked two essential factors: **source expertise and evidence sharing**. The reliability of sources requires evaluation for their reporting accuracy and their potential biases, which might affect their content and the evidence they provide.

Sam never turned into someone who doubted everything or everyone. She developed the ability to adjust her information trust levels according to the quality of its sources. She accepted claims from trustworthy sources with specialized knowledge right away but approached claims from unreliable sources with doubt, followed by deeper investigation.

The lessons from Sam demonstrate that possessing detective skills remains vital for both smart decision-making and understanding the world because information spreads through misinformation while complex truths exist in abundance.

Chapter Summary

Sam's carrot and night vision investigation proves that truth detective work extends beyond collecting facts because it needs source understanding and source evaluation and proper question development. Good detectives track claims back to their sources while consulting experts and verifying multiple reliable sources before changing their minds when they find superior evidence. The practice of being a truth detective continues throughout life because it enables us to handle complex information in our daily news consumption and social media usage and everyday conversations.

Chapter 5:
Making Good
Choices When
You're Not Sure

L ily Park stood before two flyers on her desk, which caused her uncertainty she had never faced throughout her ten years. Why was she feeling like this, and what could be done about it? Both activities were fantastic starting next week and shared the same meeting time on Tuesday afternoon. She had to choose, and it wasn't going to be easy. The difficulty of choosing weighed on her because she didn't have sufficient details to decide which option would prove best for her. And she did want to have the better one, and now she had to choose.

The first flyer used bright green colors with robot-building and computer programming images of children. The headline read "Robotics Club: Build the Future!" Members would gain skills to design and construct their robots before programming them to solve challenges and entering regional tournaments against rival schools. What an opportunity! Building robotic devices that could function and think independently fascinated Lily because she had always been interested in computer mechanisms. Who could help her decide? It was very upsetting; it was an experience she didn't want.

The deep-blue flyer showed kids performing theatrical acts under stage lights. The advertisement read, "Drama Club: Discover Your Voice!" The description outlined that club participants would gain acting skills and unite to stage performances, which would be in front of family and friends. Lily enjoyed storytelling activities because she always found pleasure in reading aloud and performing book scenes in class. Both of them were something she loved.

The two activities matched perfectly with different aspects of her personality. Lily showed aptitude for building and solving puzzles, which indicated she would enjoy robotics. She expressed both creativity and a love for performing for others, which indicated she should join the drama club. She lacked practical experience in either activity, so she couldn't determine which path would lead to greater long-term satisfaction.

The situation became more difficult because *several of her friends insisted on their preferred activities for her.* Maya, who was Lily's closest friend, had enrolled in the robotics club and continuously mentioned how wonderful it would be to have her as part of their team. The previous year, Carlos had been in a drama club as he entered his senior year and continuously praised the enjoyment of performing on stage. The good intentions of her friends created more conflict between the two activities she wanted to pursue. She was feeling anxious, with the sense of being pushed and pulled in two different directions.

Lily expressed her worries to her mother about making the programming choice in robotics club at dinner. She was concerned about joining the drama club because she feared she might develop stage fright, which would prevent her from performing in front of others.

That night, her mom took a seat beside her on the bed. "*The concerns you have are completely understandable, sweetheart. I have a question for you: Is it possible for anyone to know exactly how their decision's outcome will be before taking action?*"

Lily thought about this. She understood that all essential decisions she could remember contained elements of uncertainty. The family had no way of predicting how they would fit in when they moved into their present home two years ago. She had not predicted her success or pleasure with the school soccer team when she first tried out for it. Every decision she made, from selecting her school outfit to picking a new book, *involved unpredictable results.*

Most decisions include unknown elements, according to Lily. "*This decision holds great significance to me since I am scared about picking the wrong path.*"

Her mom nodded understandingly. She told her that it felt crucial at this moment, yet it was natural to seek the best decision. There could be multiple correct choices instead of one right answer, according to what she told Lily. *Both choices would produce positive experiences,* even though they would be different from one another.

Understanding Decision-Making Under Uncertainty

Lily accepted her mother's advice about how normal it is to *experience discomfort because of incomplete information.* Most significant life choices require individuals to make decisions while lacking complete knowledge about their future outcomes. Although complete information may be impossible to obtain, decision-making involves using available information while *tolerating uncertain outcomes.*

The main objective, according to her mom, was not to get rid of uncertainty since it was impossible to eliminate. Your primary goal should be to select the best possible decision from the information you currently possess.

Lily discovered several methods of making solid choices even when future outcomes remained unpredictable. The essential thing to do was *concentrate on things she knew* instead of losing focus on things she could not predict.

Since Lily could not determine her robotics or drama talent, she focused on which activity she preferred as an initial step. She should examine her previous encounters with comparable activities. And she needed to analyze her future aspirations and personal values while selecting the option that matched her desired self-image.

Gathering Available Information

Lily started by obtaining all the relevant information she could access before deciding. The process involved verifying that she possessed all accessible data instead of attempting to reduce uncertainty.

Lily spoke directly with the robotics and drama club teachers to get detailed information about what members would have to do. The robotics club leader, Mrs. Rodriguez, stated that robotics experience was not required since the club existed to teach absolute beginners. The club focused on teamwork and creative problem-solving, together with technical skills, according to her.

The drama club under Mr. Johnson's leadership focused equally on building confidence and communication skills and acting abilities, according to what he told Lily. The team made sure that all performers received proper support to feel comfortable while performing, since no student was required to take part in roles that exceeded their comfort level. His explanation was reassuring.

The information Lily received helped to solve some of the particular concerns she had regarding each club's activity. The clubs welcomed new members while focusing on gradual skill development for their participants.

Lily watched both clubs perform their activities as part of her decision-making process. The robotics club meeting allowed her to see students her age working together to program small robots that navigated obstacle courses. The environment was marked by a collaborative spirit and enjoyable problem-solving discussions among members.

Lily joined Mr. Johnson's drama club to watch their rehearsal performance of upcoming scenes. She found the group to be highly supportive while observing how they delighted in bringing their characters to life through teamwork. This too was a reassuring activity that she would feel comfortable joining.

Creating a Decision-Making Framework

Lily obtained more information yet she remained unsure about making a decision between her options. Both clubs presented themselves as enjoyable experiences with effective management systems. The programs provided essential learning opportunities to students. Both programs provided her with chances to meet new friends and develop herself through fresh experiences. There are so many good things about each program that it increased her concern about making a decision.

Lily's mom proposed the **Choice Chart** approach as a solution to stop her from making a decision through constant worrying. The Choice Chart would help her analyze her choices better.

The Choice Chart Method

The Choice Chart process required Lily to complete specific steps, which helped her structure her thinking during the decision-making process.

Before evaluating the two options against each other, Lily dedicated time to identifying what matters most to her. She wanted to understand the advantages she would obtain from an extracurricular activity. What type of experiences did she find most important in her life?

Lily chose an activity because it would help her gain new abilities while fostering teamwork with others, promoting creative development, and enhancing her self-assurance. She needed an activity that would be both enjoyable and interesting rather than additional academic work.

During her assessment of the robotics club, Lily found multiple attractive features, including technology learning and programming experience, hands-on work and problem-solving abilities, tournament competition and time with her best friend Maya.

Step 1: Clarify Your Values and Goals: She found different beneficial elements in drama club, which included building speaking confidence in public and learning about storytelling and theatrical arts and production work and theatrical performance knowledge and stepping out of her comfort zone. It would be a major change for Lily, but she felt deep down that it would be best for her.

Step 2: List the Positive Aspects of Each Option: Lily attempted to identify realistic benefits that each choice might present during this phase. The technical aspects of robotics club concerned her because they might become difficult to handle if she lacked natural aptitude.

Step 3: Consider the Potential Drawbacks: The main worry she had about drama club participation was her concern about performing in front of public audiences. She also had doubts about missing out on acquiring technical skills that could prove useful in a future career.

Step 4: Think About Alignment with Long-Term Interests: Lily evaluated which choice would better fit with her long-term goals

and interests. The activities she enjoyed both creatively and analyti-
cally made each option seem suitable for her future growth.

Step 5: Consider the Reversibility of the Decision: Lily, together with her mother, evaluated if the current decision was permanent or if she could transition to a different path when needed.
During their discussion, they learned *she could enroll in only one club
this semester,* yet she could join the alternative club the next semester
if she changed.

Making Peace with Imperfect Information

After filling out the Choice Chart, Lily gained an essential understanding that both alternatives possessed real value and that either choice would create beneficial experiences. The understanding
brought *both comfort and disappointment to her.* The knowledge that
her decision did not involve choosing between good and bad options
brought comfort, but it made her frustrated because there might not
be one obvious right choice.

Lily understood the source of her decision-making struggles as she
spoke to her mother. *"It's not that one choice is right and one is wrong.
They're both good choices in different ways."*

Her mom smiled. *"That's very mature insight. The majority of challenging life choices present as difficult decisions between good alternatives instead of between good and bad options."*

Lily's mom explained to her that the actual choice between options
became less important than *the method she used to make that decision.*
Through her systematic approach of value consideration and information collection and balanced evaluation, *Lily built decision-making
abilities* that would benefit her throughout her entire life.

The Final Decision

Lily noticed that the drama club now seemed more appealing to her
after finishing her analysis. The creative and performance elements of

the drama club deeply attracted her, even though the rational evaluation did not clearly support her interest. But, she knew she would be able to overcome her fear of performing before an audience, and that was a major plus for her.

Lily announced to her family during dinner that she wanted to enroll in drama club. "*I want to join drama club because the idea fascinates me right* now, *even though I* believe the *robotics club might be equally good.*"

Her dad asked her to explain why she had chosen the drama club instead of participating in robotics activities. "*It wasn't really about deciding against robotics,*" she said. "*The decision I made was about* **choosing to face my fears** *by attempting something that makes me uncomfortable yet gives me a thrill. The opportunity to try robotics club remains available to me during the upcoming semester if I decide to take it.*"

The first reaction Maya had toward Lily not participating in robotics club with her was negative, yet she appreciated the thorough approach Lily before deciding. Because Maya had seen nothing like it, Lily's **chart impressed her.** "*The way she presents her decision is unique, so I need to try that method when I face challenging decisions.*"

Learning from the Decision Process

After joining drama club, Lily spent weeks analyzing the lessons she learned from her decision-making experience. She discovered that the process she used to decide had equal value compared to the outcome of the decision.

Key Insights About Decision-Making

A person can reach good decisions even when they have imperfect information. Lily discovered that postponing to achieve complete certainty typically results in permanent indecision. The objective was to acquire adequate information in choosing the best decision *based on the available data*.

Different options can be equally good choices. Lily learned to embrace multiple positive outcomes instead of trying to identify one exclusive perfect solution during her decision process. She also learned that *there is no perfect solution* to anything and that there may be several acceptable solutions.

The practice of decision-making becomes better through experience. Through this structured decision process, Lily learned an approach that she could use for upcoming choices regardless of their magnitude.

Decisions should be *based on personal values together with established goals*. Lily discovered how to assess her choices against her fundamental values as well as her future-oriented objectives when making decisions.

Decisions that can be undone carry lower risks. This decision became less permanent and stressful because Lily realized she could try robotics club at some point in the future.

Applying the Skills to Everyday Choices

Lily used her decision-making structure to help her navigate other life situations after she started enjoying her work at drama club. She used a basic version of her Choice Chart to analyze various book options for her school project.

She also proposed developing a family Choice Chart to assess summer vacation destinations when her family needed to decide their trip location. Her parents appreciated her structured decision-making method because the exercise made their discussions about preferences and priorities more effective.

Next, Lily began providing assistance to her friends whenever they needed help with important choices. Lily supported Maya by asking her to determine her party goals and select the theme that would create the most enjoyment for her birthday celebration. She advised Carlos to think about his goals and gather information about time commitment before assessing whether joining the school basketball team aligned with his other interests.

Growing Comfortable with Uncertainty

Lily gained the ability to handle unknown situations as her most significant learning from this experience. She understood that uncertainty about decisions does not automatically indicate poor choices or the need for additional information. The process of deciding about future matters sometimes creates natural periods of uncertainty.

The decision-making process did not make Lily neglect proper information gathering or become reckless in her choices. She developed skills to differentiate between helpful uncertainty, which encouraged her to think and obtain proper data, and unhelpful uncertainty, which caused continuous doubt and prevented decision-making.

Lily understood that some of her most significant experiences emerged from uncertain decisions. The positive outcome of joining drama club proved to be excellent, yet she understood that predicting this result beforehand had been impossible. By taking decisive actions despite uncertain outcomes, she uncovered new possibilities that would have remained hidden if she had demanded absolute clarity before making decisions.

The Ongoing Journey

As Lily spent more time with the drama club, she became certain that she had selected the correct activity. The creative elements of the club, combined with her new friendships and enhanced communication abilities and performance skills, proved very valuable to her.

The robotics club caught Lily's attention, so she planned to join it during the upcoming semester. The decision she made didn't prevent her from exploring additional options, but it specified what she would do during this specific time period.

Most importantly, Lily discovered that the skills she had developed for making this decision about after-school activities were transferable to many other areas of life. Students who want to succeed should learn to clarify their values while gathering relevant information to help them weigh the pros and cons of their decisions. Before you start your search for relevant data, stop trying to eliminate uncertainty.

Make sure to evaluate *all choices based on their advantages and disadvantages* and match them to your targets and personal values before considering adjustment or reversal options. A proper decision involves utilizing available information to make a thoughtful choice, which leads to confident movement toward your objectives.

Chapter Summary

The experience of Lily selecting robotics club or drama club shows that good decision-making requires accepting uncertainty instead of trying to remove it. Lily's decision was carefully made, considering unknown outcomes, as she established values, gathered data, and evaluated options. The Choice Chart method enables people to think more effectively about decisions by focusing on known facts instead of unknown factors.

Chapter 6:
Explaining Your
Ideas Clearly

A lex Kumar dedicated three weeks to developing what he firmly believed would become the best fourth-grade science project ever made. Through his working model, he showed how chlorophyll and solar energy help convert carbon dioxide and water into glucose and oxygen in the process of photosynthesis. The project used LED lights and colored water and plastic tubing to show the complete process in its different stages through a complex chamber setup.

Alex completely understood every aspect of his project functionality. He could detail chemical reactions while explaining each component function and explain why photosynthesis sustains Earth's living organisms. He studied what seemed like a mountain of articles and watched educational videos and spoke with a botanist at the local university for his research. The project existed perfectly in his mind, and he believed it would wow everyone at the upcoming science fair.

Then Alex made his presentation to his family the evening before the science fair. He displayed his elaborate setup while standing beside it before delivering his practiced speech.

"Good evening, distinguished guests. During this presentation, I will explain photosynthesis by describing the light-dependent reactions in thylakoid membranes and the Calvin cycle, which happens in chloroplast stroma," Alex started confidently.

He observed his parents exchanging puzzled expressions at that moment. Six-year-old Mindy completely failed to understand what was happening. His thirty-year-teaching grandmother struggled to understand the explanation while Alex presented it.

Alex described the function of photosystem I and photosystem II along with the electron transport chain and ATP and NADPH production. He used advanced scientific terms like "chemiosmosis" and "rubisco enzyme," and "carbon fixation" with exactness to show off his scientific terminology skills. This was a problem, not for Alex but for his audience.

Following his five-minute talk, *the audience maintained complete silence* for a brief period. His dad interrupted the silence with a gentle throat clearing.

"Your presentation was extensive, but I found it challenging to follow until the end, Alex," his father explained. *"Your knowledge about photosynthesis stands out because* you show *an extensive comprehension of this process. The information you presented went over my head, and it seemed I needed a science degree to grasp your project."*

A wave of anxiety swept through Alex's body. The extensive research and presentation preparation had paid off because he mastered scientific terminology and precise details about his project. He didn't understand why his family members failed to recognize the extensive work he dedicated to studying this complicated subject.

His mother took a seat beside him on the couch. *"Your project is remarkable, and your knowledge of photosynthesis exceeds expectations. Tomorrow you will present to different age groups, including scientists and parents and community members and younger children who may not understand scientific terminology."*

Alex's grandmother, who had taught elementary school for many years, provided him with some supportive advice. Being intelligent requires more than understanding complex concepts, she taught her students during her teaching career. Sharing knowledge in a way that enables others to understand it stands equally important to having knowledge itself.

According to his grandmother, Alex had mastered photosynthesis at a deep level; however, his presentation methods could actually reduce the audience's understanding of that knowledge. *Listeners who can't understand explanations from speakers usually doubt that the speaker understands* the material enough to explain it simply.

"But I do understand it!" Alex protested. *"The time I spent studying the scientific terms and their connections in the system took weeks to complete. People should be amazed by my command of complex vocabulary because I spent time learning it."*

His grandmother nodded in agreement and understanding. *"Your commitment to research shines through in your ability to master complex scientific terms. The actual difficulty lies in **applying this knowledge to teach others new concepts**. This ability represents a different skill, which matches the importance of scientific understanding."*

The intense focus on showing off his knowledge made Alex forget what his audience needed to learn from his presentation. Most of the people attending his science fair showed a casual interest in science yet lacked expertise beyond basic knowledge, so he needed to present differently from what he would do in a graduate-level biology class.

Learning to Translate Complex Ideas

The family dedicated their evening to helping Alex develop strategies for transforming his presentation. Rather than starting from the beginning, they focused on translating his intricate understanding into language and illustrations that could be comprehended by a broader audience.

His mom proposed starting with the fundamental question. *"What is photosynthesis and why should people find it important?"*

Alex took a brief pause to think. *"Plants create their nourishment along with oxygen through photosynthesis,"* he explained. *"Without it, nothing on Earth could survive."*

His dad nodded enthusiastically. *"Now that's something I can understand! Can you tell me more about that?"*

Using basic language helped Alex deliver his concepts more effectively to his audience. The explanation of plants as "amazing factories" brought new enthusiasm to his presentation. *"Plants receive sunlight along with water and carbon dioxide which we exhale to create sugar which nourishes plants and oxygen which we need to breathe."*

During Alex's original presentation, Mindy had maintained complete silence until he began his alternative explanation. She asked with real interest, *"So plants make our air?"*

"Exactly!" Alex expressed his excitement through his voice as he replied to her question. *"Every time you inhale, oxygen enters your lungs from photosynthetic plants. Small marine organisms, alongside large forest trees, produce oxygen, which forms the oxygen we inhale."*

Alex's grandmother pointed out something important. *"Your approach with this alternative explanation transformed Mindy's level of interest into complete attention. Your delivery provided her with information that related directly to her everyday world. Everyone understands breathing, so when you show how plants generate the air we breathe, they can immediately recognize the importance of photosynthesis for themselves."*

Building Bridges with Examples and Analogies

Alex found out that **analogies** and examples proved to be **strong tools for teaching complex concepts** to others while he worked on his presentation. The description of plants as *"tiny green factories inside their leaves"* with *"special rooms where different parts of the work happen"* replaced his technical language about "chloroplast stroma" and "thylakoid membranes." This is where both a dictionary and a thesaurus can help you when you're reading or planning to make presentations, just like the use of analogies helped Alex.

Alex used solar panels on houses as an analogy to explain how plants capture sunlight since both convert sunlight into usable energy forms. The analogy provided a clear understanding of this concept to people who didn't require the chemical details about how chlorophyll absorbs photons. Simple can always be best when explaining complex concepts, so keep this in mind.

Young children can understand the carbon dioxide and oxygen exchange by using the analogy that Alex presented. His explanation showed that plants and people maintain a friendly relationship through mutual sharing of their requirements. The carbon dioxide plants receive from our breath creates oxygen, which we need to survive. It's like the perfect trade.

The elaborate model gained more effectiveness when Alex used it to create a narrative instead of merely highlighting technical aspects. Through his explanation, he *guided viewers through the process* of how water moves from roots to leaves and how sunlight converts basic elements into nutritional products and oxygen. He was making science simpler and easier to understand with words that presented visuals to his audience. In effect, Alex was also exhibiting humility in that he didn't need to appear smarter than his audience, and his presentation benefited from this.

Practicing the Art of Clear Communication

The next morning, Alex felt anxious yet well-prepared while he arranged his display at the science fair. After several practice sessions, he was becoming skilled at modifying his explanations for his audience.

Alex received his first visitors when second-graders along with their teacher visited his booth. Alex lowered his body to meet the students at their height level. He asked the audience whether any of them had ever experienced hunger. The entire group of children lifted their hands. *"Plants experience hunger just like humans do, but they lack the ability to seek snacks in refrigerators. Plants produce their food using sunlight and water in combination with air. Would you like to see their food production process?"*

The children paid close attention as Alex showed his model using basic terms while asking interactive questions to maintain their interest. He pointed to the green water while asking if anyone could explain the process that occurs when light shines on it. He activated his LED lighting system to demonstrate his point. The colored water within the tubes captured the children's attention as they observed its movement, because the tubes simulated how materials are distributed in a plant.

The second-graders left to explore other displays, but Alex received a surge of motivation from their genuine understanding and enthusiasm. A new group of high school students came to stand before his display shortly afterward. The audience change happened automatically as Alex moved from basic language to more complex terms yet maintained straightforward explanations.

"The process that you observe in this display is named photosynthesis," he said. *"Plants transform light energy into chemical energy by creating*

glucose for food production while simultaneously releasing oxygen as a byproduct." Through his model, he demonstrated the process of water and carbon dioxide entering the system while chlorophyll in leaves absorbs solar energy to start chemical transformations.

Adapting to Different Audiences

Throughout the day, Alex noticed that his presentation style evolved automatically to suit various groups. He'd ask older visitors about gardening before connecting photosynthesis to their plant care. The environmental value of photosynthesis stood out to him when discussing this with parents who had children. Now he was beginning to realize the rhythm of adapting to the audience's knowledge and wish for information.

A woman who used a wheelchair came toward his exhibit together with her daughter. The high position of his model caused a problem for him, so he brought some components down to a lower table while he moved to have a better conversation with her.

The woman pointed to her daughter and said, "*My daughter keeps asking about the reason behind leaf color.*" In response, Alex said, "*You were hoping someone would help with this explanation.*"

The young girl noted Alex smiled before he began his explanation. "*That's a great question! Leaves obtain their green color from chlorophyll, which functions as a green pigment that absorbs sunlight. Chlorophyll serves two purposes since it provides leaves with their green appearance and enables plants to convert sunlight into nutritional substances.*"

The girl's eyes widened with understanding. The processing of leaves, light, and food resulted in their green appearance. It all made sense to her.

The mother was very appreciative of Alex for his simple explanation. She confirmed that she worked as a science teacher at the local high school. "*You have an exceptional skill to explain complicated concepts to everyone successfully,*" she said. "*You have shown the potential to teach others. Does the thought of becoming a teacher interest you?*" It hadn't occurred to Alex, but now he reconsidered his career options.

Learning from Feedback

The science fair judges, together with teachers and visitors, provided feedback to Alex, which helped him determine the factors that made his presentation effective. Multiple observers appreciated *how he adjusted his explanations to fit diverse audiences* without affecting their level of understanding or reducing essential information.

A judge at the fair specifically pointed out that Alex performed exceptionally well when using analogies. She mentioned that he made photosynthesis more accessible than any textbook she had encountered. "*Your description of plants as factories and their connection to people made both processes easier to understand and remember.*"

The feedback that Alex received provided him with constructive advice to help improve his work. The teacher proposed drawing a basic chemical equation diagram for photosynthesis to enhance its model's effectiveness. The observation shows that *combining visual information with verbal explanations enhances knowledge comprehension for various learners.*

Discovering the Joy of Teaching

After interacting with many people about photosynthesis at the science fair, Alex discovered that his *experience of teaching was equally rewarding to him* as was his research work and model construction. The process of teaching new concepts to students brought him deep satisfaction because it led to their comprehension and their curiosity about science. Curiosity, he knew, was an excellent tool to initiate exploration and learn.

Alex learned that *scientific knowledge combined with good communication abilities* created powerful learning experiences. His thorough comprehension of photosynthesis produced precise and certain explanations, but his advancing communication skills delivered this knowledge in an understandable format for others. It was a win-win situation.

During the winner announcement, Alex discovered that his category position placed him in second place. The development of his skills as both a scientist and a communicator stood as his most important achievement to him during this entire project.

The Ripple Effect of Clear Communication

Alex employed his new communication skills in various situations during the weeks following the science fair. He demonstrated math concepts through game-related examples when assisting his sister with her homework. He also assisted his friend Marcus with a history lesson on the American Revolution by transforming historical dates and facts into *story-based explanations* that included characters, conflicts, and motivations.

By becoming a tutor for younger students at his school, Alex discovered that teaching others strengthened his comprehension of the subjects he taught. When he needed to explain concepts to others in a way they would understand, he frequently discovered important knowledge gaps that required his attention. Now he knew that every teacher faced new challenges when they came across information that they didn't have adequate knowledge of themselves. It meant that they would have to explore further to strengthen what they knew to where they could make it simpler for others to understand. He also knew that if you truly didn't have solid knowledge of something, you couldn't simply explain it to others.

The teaching staff at school noticed that Alex displayed better communication abilities during classroom discussions and presentations. Alex focused on delivering his ideas clearly and making new concepts accessible to his classmates instead of using advanced vocabulary to display his knowledge. His improved communication skills made him more important for group projects as well as in class discussions.

The Building Blocks of Clear Communication

Alex learned through his science fair experience and additional practice that several core principles help people effectively communicate complex ideas.

Know Your Audience

Alex discovered that every explanation should begin with *assessing the audience knowledge level* about the subject. His explanations for kindergarten students required simpler vocabulary and different examples than those for high school students, even though they studied the same fundamental concepts.

Start with the Big Picture

Before entering detailed technical aspects, Alex developed the practice of *beginning with essential or captivating elements of his subject.* Photosynthesis begins with demonstrating its significance for Earth's living organisms instead of starting with molecular details.

Use Familiar Examples and Analogies

People could understand new concepts more easily when Alex *demonstrated them through comparisons to familiar things.* The explanation of *plants as factories* together with *chlorophyll as solar panels* helped people build mental connections for understanding complex information.

Check for Understanding

During his presentations, Alex observed the audience's reactions to gauge their understanding of his explanations and asked questions to assess their comprehension level. The moment he saw someone look confused, he shifted his approach to explain the concept differently. He also began asking his audience questions to test their understanding of what he was presenting.

Show Genuine Enthusiasm

The genuine excitement that Alex felt about photosynthesis proved to be highly contagious to his audience. His *genuine passion* for the information made people become more interested in and invested in the topic.

Practice Active Listening

Alex developed his *listening skills by paying close attention* to people's questions and comments to provide accurate answers instead of following his scripted presentation. Through this approach, conversations became more give-and-take and beneficial for all participants.

Building Confidence Through Practice

Through his communication practice, Alex found that simple explanations of concepts resulted in better comprehension of the material for himself. Through breaking down complex ideas and finding effective analogies, he got better insights into how different concepts relate to each other. He was learning himself now and extending his understanding of his subject.

Learning to communicate clearly helped Alex understand that explaining concepts to others simultaneously *strengthened his thinking abilities* and tested his comprehension. Simple explanations of information revealed his need to *spend more time thinking about it*. Alex began *asking himself how he could better explain something* or make it simpler to understand, and he was benefiting.

Chapter Summary

The transformation of Alex from using technical scientific language to developing clear and suitable communication shows that genuine comprehension *requires the ability to explain complex ideas in understandable ways*. Effective communication demands that you *understand your audience first* and *begin with broad ideas* while incorporating *common analogies* and examples and verifying understanding while maintaining authentic enthusiasm for your material. The power of simple explanation goes beyond educational support because it allows you to deepen your knowledge while structuring your mental processes. Communication skills develop better with experience and constructive feedback, which improves educational learning and teaching experiences for all participants. All of us, in one way or another, will be teachers in our lives, even if we never go into the teaching profession. We will teach our friends, families, neighbors, or schoolmates.

Chapter 7:
Working with
Smart Computers

Zoe Washington stared at her math homework with a mixture of frustration and exhaustion. It was Thursday evening, and she had been working on word problems for over an hour. Some problems seemed impossibly complicated, with multiple steps and confusing language that made her head spin. She didn't know whether she could do it. Stress was really getting to her now, and she wasn't sure what she should do.

"A train leaves Station A traveling at 65 miles per hour," she read aloud from problem number twelve. *"Another train leaves Station B, which is 300 miles away, traveling toward Station A at 55 miles per hour. If both trains leave, when will they meet?"*

Zoe groaned and put her head down on her desk. She had solved the first eleven problems with great effort, but this one seemed completely different from anything they had practiced in class. She understood the individual concepts—she could multiply and divide, and she knew what speed and distance meant, but putting it all together felt over-whelming.

Her brother Tyler, who was working on his homework nearby, noticed her distress. "*Having trouble*?" he asked sympathetically.

"*This problem doesn't make any sense,*" Zoe complained. "*Why would anyone need to know when two trains meet? And how am I supposed to figure out something that involves two different speeds and times and distances all at once?*"

Tyler came over to look at her homework. "*You know,*" he said thoughtfully, "*I've been using this really cool computer program to help with my science research. It's like having a* super-smart *study buddy that can explain things and help solve problems. Want to try it?*"

Zoe was curious. She knew about computer programs that could answer questions and help with homework, but she hadn't tried using one. Tyler showed her how to access the program on their family computer and explained how to ask it questions to get helpful responses.

"*Just type in your problem and **ask it to explain how to solve it**,*" Tyler suggested. "*It's like having a teacher available whenever you need help.*" He also explained how a specific website on the Internet had helped him learn much of what he knew about computers and learning. It was *the Khan Academy.*

Zoe carefully typed in the train problem and *asked the computer to help her understand how to solve it.* **She wasn't asking it to give her the answer,** but to help her understand how to solve the problem. Within seconds, she had a detailed response that *broke the problem down into manageable steps*. The program explained that this was called a "relative speed" problem and showed her a formula she could use to find the answer. Zoe now had the answer for the steps she could use to solve the problem herself. In other words, she was learning how to do something thanks to the program's instructions.

"*Wow!*" Zoe exclaimed as she read through the explanation. "*This makes so much more sense now. The computer even drew a little diagram showing how the trains are moving toward each other.*" Visuals were very helpful because Zoe knows now that *this type of information is easier for her to understand* than written information. And she wasn't alone because many other students discovered that visual presentations were much easier for them to understand, too.

Following the program's guidance, Zoe could solve the problem correctly. She felt a rush of satisfaction and relief. This computer helper was amazing; it was just as her brother had said, like having a personal tutor who was always patient and never made her feel stupid for asking questions.

The Temptation of Easy Answers

Excited by her success with the train problem, Zoe decided to ask the computer program for help with the remaining math problems on her worksheet. One by one, she typed in each problem and received clear, step-by-step solutions. Within twenty minutes, she had completed an assignment that might have taken her hours to finish on her own. And, best of all, *she understood what she was doing, why it was being done, and how to arrive at the correct answer.*

As Zoe closed her math book with a sense of accomplishment, she began thinking about how this computer helper could transform her homework routine. Why struggle with difficult problems when she could get instant help and explanations? Could she save time by asking the computer to summarize the information instead of spending hours reading and researching? But she knew it might also be helpful to read the original information and then the summary that the computer program provided to her.

The next day at school, Zoe's math teacher, Mrs. Patterson, returned their graded homework assignments. Zoe was thrilled to see that she had received a perfect score on the problems she had completed with the computer's help. She felt proud and confident as she compared her grade to those of her classmates, some of whom had struggled with the same problems she had found so challenging.

That afternoon, Zoe faced another homework challenge, and this time in social studies. She needed to write a short report about the American Civil War, including information about its causes, major battles, and consequences. Rather than spending time reading through her textbook and researching additional sources, Zoe decided to ask her computer helper to write the report with her.

The computer quickly generated a well-organized, informative report that covered all the required topics. The writing was clear and poiished, and it included details that Zoe hadn't learned in class yet. She was impressed by how much the computer seemed to "know" and how well it could organize information.

Zoe copied the computer-generated report into her own document, made a few small changes to make it sound more like her own writing style, and submitted it the next day, feeling confident about her work.

A Surprising Discovery

When Mrs. Chen, Zoe's social studies teacher, returned the reports the following week, Zoe was surprised and confused by the feedback she received. While her grade was decent, Mrs. Chen had written several comments in the margins that didn't make sense to Zoe.

"Excellent point about the economic factors, but can you explain what you mean by 'industrial paradigm shifts'?" one comment read. *"This seems like advanced analysis. Where did this insight come from?"*

Another comment noted, *"The section about the Battle of Antietam includes details we haven't covered in class. What sources did you use for this information?"*

Zoe realized with growing anxiety that she couldn't answer any of Mrs. Chen's questions. She had no idea what "industrial paradigm shifts" meant, even though those words appeared in her report. She couldn't explain the details of the Battle of Antietam because she hadn't actually learned about it; the computer had included that information without her understanding or input.

But Zoe was filled with dread when Mrs. Chen asked to speak with her after class.

"Zoe," Mrs. Chen said gently, *"I'm concerned about your report. The writing quality and analysis level seem quite different from your usual work, and some of the information included doesn't match what we've been studying. Can you help me understand how you approached this assignment?"*

Her face burned with embarrassment as she realized she had to be honest about using the computer helper. She explained how she had asked the program to write the report for her, thinking it would help her learn the material more efficiently.

Mrs. Chen listened thoughtfully and didn't seem angry, which surprised Zoe. *"I appreciate your honesty,"* she said. *"And I understand the appeal of having a computer do difficult work for you. But I'm worried that you might be missing out on some important learning opportunities."*

Understanding the Difference Between Help and Replacement

Mrs. Chen sat down beside Zoe and helped her think about the difference between *using technology as a helpful tool versus using it as a replacement* for her own thinking and learning.

"Computers can be incredible learning partners," Mrs. Chen explained. *"They can help you find information, explain difficult concepts,*

and even check your work. But when we let them do our thinking for us, we miss out on developing our own understanding and skills."

She helped Zoe understand that *learning wasn't just about getting the right answers* but that it was about developing the ability to think through problems, analyze information, and express ideas in her own words. When the computer wrote her report for her, Zoe had missed out on the process of reading about the Civil War, forming her own understanding of the events, and practicing how to organize and communicate her thoughts.

"Think about it this way," Mrs. Chen said. *"If you always let a calculator do your math for you, you might get correct answers, but you wouldn't develop your own math skills. Similarly, if you always let a computer do your writing and research for you, you won't develop your own thinking and communication abilities."* It was an important lesson that Zoe was learning.

Zoe began to see the problem. While the computer had helped her complete her assignments quickly, *it hadn't helped her actually learn the material* or develop her own skills. When Mrs. Chen asked her questions about her report, Zoe realized that she didn't really understand what she had submitted.

"So should I never use the computer helper?" Zoe asked, worried that she had been doing something completely wrong.

Mrs. Chen smiled. *"Not at all! The key is learning how to use it as a thinking partner rather than a replacement for your own thinking. Let me show you what I mean."*

Learning to Collaborate with Technology

Mrs. Chen helped Zoe understand that the most effective way to work with smart computer programs was to use them in working partnerships in the learning process, rather than as tools that eliminated the need for her own thinking.

For her math homework, this meant using the computer to *help her understand concepts* and check her work, but still doing the actual problem-solving herself. Instead of asking the computer to solve problems for her, Zoe could *ask it to explain the steps involved*, provide similar examples, or help her understand why certain approaches worked. It was exactly what she had done earlier when the computer program provided all of the steps so that she not only understood but could also follow the steps to solve the math problems.

For research and writing assignments, Zoe could use the computer to help her find information, understand difficult concepts, and organize her thoughts, but the actual analysis and writing should come from her own understanding and perspective. This would increase her understanding of the subject about which she was writing.

"The computer is like a very knowledgeable study buddy," Mrs. Chen explained. *"A good study buddy can help you understand material and check your thinking, but they shouldn't do your homework for you. The goal is for both of you to learn and grow together."* In fact, Mrs. Chen helped her understand that some programs could even keep instructions in memory so that when she came back, she could have the program work with her on something in memory. Yes, even the computer program was learning something about her and her writing style. She even went further than that because she told her she could speak to the computer and the program would understand what she was saying and type it out.

Mrs. Chen suggested that Zoe try rewriting her Civil War report using the computer as a collaborative partner rather than a replacement. This time, instead of asking the computer to write the report for her, Zoe could ask it to help her understand specific concepts, suggest good sources for research, and provide feedback on her writing.

The Revision Process

Excited to try this new approach, Zoe started over with her Civil War report. This time, she began by reading the relevant chapter in her textbook and taking her notes about the causes, events, and consequences of the war.

When she encountered concepts that were difficult to understand, such as the economic differences between the North and South, she asked the computer to explain these ideas in simpler terms. The computer provided helpful explanations that made the material more accessible, but Zoe took the time to understand the explanations and put the information into her own words.

When she was ready to write, Zoe created her own outline based on her notes and understanding. She then asked the computer program to review her outline and suggest improvements. The program pointed out that she might want to include more information about how the war affected ordinary people, not just political and military leaders.

As Zoe wrote each section of her report, she periodically asked the computer to check her facts and suggest areas where she could provide more detail or better organization. When the computer suggested that she include information about specific battles, Zoe took the time to research those battles herself and understand why they were significant.

The process took longer than simply asking the computer to write the report for her, but Zoe found it much more helpful. She was learning about the Civil War in depth, developing her own insights about the topic, and improving her writing skills at the same time.

Discovering What Humans and Computers Do Best

Through her experience with the computer helper, Zoe began to understand that humans and computers each had different strengths that could complement each other. Computers have been trained by people who wrote algorithms (programs) that help craft questions for the computer to then go and seek answers to these questions.

What Computers Do Well

Zoe learned that computers were excellent at *storing and retrieving huge amounts of information quickly.* They can perform calculations rapidly and quickly identify patterns in data and provide detailed explanations of complex topics. They were also available whenever she needed help and never got impatient with repeated questions.

Computers have **one major fault**, and everybody must understand it. What is the fault? *It's called **hallucinating***, and it means that a computer program will make up an answer in response to your question. *These answers may not be correct,* so *you have to go back to check them*. This occurs particularly when users are looking for **specific articles or URLs**. Let's look at this in a different way.

The brain functions in a special way when someone is exhausted or when they have an intense dream. Your brain creates perceptions of things that don't exist while your mind adds missing details to incomplete information.

Computers possess the **ability to create similar effects to human hallucinations**. A computer hallucinates when it *generates false information* that appears authentic but lacks actual truth. The computer's "brain" experiences confusion, which leads it to *make guesses* instead of providing certain answers. It almost sounds human, but we have to remember that the programs are intended to answer what we've requested of them.

The question was, "*What color was George Washington's pet dragon?*" would receive a fabricated response from a hallucinating computer as "*bright blue with golden spots.*" Why? The computer produced this false information because *it attempted to provide an answer despite George Washington never owning a dragon as a pet.* The program will respond to you, even if it has to fabricate a reply. Sometimes it will make up URLs, and we have to go and check that that website actually exists.

It's like telling a story but forgetting certain details, leading you to replace them with incorrect or possibly false information. The computer *operates without malicious intent to deceive others,* but it does sometimes mix up real information with imaginary data.

It's always important to verify critical information no matter how believable a computer presents it to you. As most programs will tell you, be sure to verify the information provided by the computer.

The computer helper in Zoe's case was particularly good at breaking down complicated problems into smaller, manageable steps. When Zoe was confused by a math problem or couldn't understand a historical concept, the computer provided multiple explanations and examples until she found an approach that made sense to her.

These machines are also excellent at checking work for errors. They can quickly identify mathematical mistakes, spelling errors, or logical inconsistencies that might be difficult for humans to catch.

What Humans Do Best

On the other hand, Zoe discovered that humans brought unique strengths to the learning process that computers couldn't replicate. Humans were much better at understanding context, making creative connections between different ideas, and developing personal insights based on their experiences and perspectives.

Zoe realized that her curiosity, creativity, and ability to relate new information to things she already knew were irreplaceable parts of the learning process. When she read about the Civil War, she could imagine what it might have been like to live during that time, connect the historical events to current issues she cared about, and develop her own opinions about the decisions that historical figures had made.

Humans were also better at asking the right questions and knowing when something made little sense. While the computer could provide accurate information, Zoe was better at determining which information was most important for her specific assignment and which details might be confusing or irrelevant for her intended audience.

Building a Productive Partnership

As Zoe became more experienced at working with her computer helper, she developed strategies for creating productive partnerships that maximized both human and computer strengths.

1. *Ask for Explanations, Not Answers*: Instead of asking the computer to solve problems for her, Zoe learned to ask for explanations of concepts and strategies. For math problems, she would ask, "*Can you explain how to approach this type of problem?*" rather than "*What's the answer to this problem?*"

2. *Use Technology to Check Your Thinking:* After solving problems or writing drafts on her own, Zoe would ask the computer to review her work and identify potential errors or areas for improvement. This helped her catch mistakes while still requiring her to do the primary thinking and problem-solving.

3. *Seek Multiple Perspectives:* When researching topics, Zoe learned to ask the computer to provide different viewpoints or explanations rather than just accepting the first response. This helped her develop a more comprehensive understanding of complex issues.

4. *Maintain Ownership of Your Learning:* More importantly, Zoe learned to stay actively engaged in her own learning process. She would read, think, and form her own under-

standing before asking the computer for help, and she would always take time to understand and evaluate the computer's responses rather than blindly accepting them.

5. *Sharing the Discovery with Friends:* Zoe's new approach to working with technology soon caught the attention of her classmates. When her friend Marcus was struggling with a science project about renewable energy, Zoe suggested that he try using the computer helper as a collaborative partner rather than trying to complete the project entirely on his own.

Together, they developed a strategy where Marcus would first research the topic using traditional sources and develop his own basic understanding. Then he would use the computer to help clarify confusing concepts, suggest additional research directions, and review his project for accuracy and completeness.

The collaboration was so successful that Marcus asked Zoe to help him understand how she had learned to work so effectively with technology. Zoe realized that she had developed a valuable skill that could benefit other students as well.

With Mrs. Chen's encouragement, Zoe created a presentation for her class about effective collaboration with computer helpers. She shared her own experience of initially using technology as a replacement for thinking, then learning to use it as a partner instead.

"The goal isn't to avoid using computer helpers," Zoe explained to her classmates. *"They're amazing tools that can make learning easier and more fun. The goal is to use them in ways that help us become better thinkers and learners, not to replace our thinking."*

Developing Digital Wisdom

As Zoe continued using her computer helper throughout the school year, she found that her relationship with technology was constantly growing. She became more skilled at asking effective questions, better at evaluating the computer's responses, and more confident in her ability to combine computer assistance with her thinking.

Now she understood what computer experts called "**prompting**." The process of prompting involves *providing computers with precise instructions or asking them questions,* which enables them to deliver their most accurate responses. You can find some basic prompting videos on the Khan Academy's "Khanmigo" website. It's a wonderful place to start learning, and it's for kids, parents, and teachers.

Zoe also learned to recognize situations where computer help might not be appropriate or necessary. For creative writing assignments, she preferred to rely primarily on her imagination and ideas, using the computer only occasionally to help with grammar or to suggest synonyms for overused words.

For math problems that were similar to ones she had already mastered, Zoe often worked through them independently to practice and reinforce her skills, only consulting the computer when she encountered genuinely new or challenging concepts.

Understanding Limitations

Through experience, Zoe also learned that computer helpers, while incredibly capable, had important limitations. Sometimes they provided information that was technically correct but not well-suited to her specific assignment or grade level. Other times, they might not understand the context of her question and provide responses that were unhelpful or confusing.

Zoe learned to approach computer responses with the same critical thinking skills she applied to other sources of information. She would ask herself whether the computer's suggestions made sense, whether they aligned with what she had learned in class, and whether they were appropriate for her specific situation.

Most importantly, Zoe understood that while computers could help her access information and check her thinking, they couldn't replace her curiosity, creativity, and personal growth. The most meaningful learning happened when she was engaged in thinking about new ideas, making connections to her experiences, and developing her own understanding of the world.

The Ongoing Partnership

By the end of the school year, Zoe had developed a productive and sustainable relationship with technology that enhanced her learning without replacing her thinking. Her grades had improved not just because she was getting more problems right, but because she was developing a deeper understanding and better study skills.

Her teachers noticed that Zoe was asking more thoughtful questions in class, contributing more meaningful insights to discussions, and demonstrating greater confidence in her academic abilities. The computer helper had become a valuable tool in her learning toolkit, but Zoe herself remained the primary driver of her educational growth.

Zoe's experience taught her that the most powerful learning happened when human creativity and curiosity combined with computer capabilities and efficiency. Rather than viewing technology as either completely beneficial or completely harmful, she had learned to approach it thoughtfully and strategically.

And Zoe discovered that working effectively with smart computers required the same critical thinking skills that were valuable in all areas of life—**the ability to ask good questions,** evaluate information carefully, and make thoughtful decisions about when and how to use different tools and resources.

Guidelines for Productive Human-Computer Collaboration

Based on her experience, Zoe developed a set of guidelines that helped her work effectively with computer helpers while maintaining her own learning and growth.

Before Using Technology

- Start with your own thinking and understanding. Read, research, and form your own initial ideas before asking for computer assistance. This ensures that you remain actively engaged in your own learning process.

When Asking for Help

- Ask for explanations and guidance rather than completed answers. Focus on understanding concepts and strategies rather than just getting correct responses. Sometimes ask a simple question, and once it has been answered, build on that to increase the complexity of your question. The computer can do this.

While Working Together

- Stay curious and engaged. Ask follow-up questions, request clarification when something makes little sense, and think critically about the computer's suggestions. Always check any answers it provides in terms of specific online material and check the website's accuracy.

After Receiving Assistance

- Take time to understand and evaluate what the computer has provided. Make sure you can explain the concepts in your own words and that the help aligns with your learning goals.

Throughout the Process

Remember that you are the primary learner. Technology should enhance your thinking, not replace it. The goal is to become smarter and more capable, not just to complete assignments quicker.

Chapter Summary

Zoe's journey from using computer helpers as replacement tools to embracing them as collaborative partners demonstrates that technology can greatly enhance learning when used thoughtfully and strategically. The key is *understanding what humans and computers each do best*, and finding ways to combine these strengths productively.

Computers excel at providing information, performing calculations, and offering explanations, while humans bring curiosity, creativity, critical thinking, and the ability to make meaningful connections. Effective collaboration with smart computers requires maintaining active engagement in your own learning, asking for guidance rather than answers, and using technology to enhance rather than replace your own thinking and understanding. Working with computer helpers successfully *requires the same critical thinking skills that are valuable in all areas of life*.

Chapter 8: Building Better Thinking Habits

C arlos Martinez sat in his bedroom on a rainy Saturday afternoon, feeling frustrated with himself. His report card came the day before, and while his grades weren't bad, they could be better. His teacher, Mr. Kim, had written a comment that kept echoing in his mind: *"Carlos is a bright student who could benefit from more consistent effort and deeper thinking about his work."* It wasn't what he had expected, but it did reveal a few things that he knew he had to try harder on, and his parents would help.

The comment hurt because Carlos knew it was true. He often rushed through assignments without really thinking them through, made careless mistakes on tests even when he understood the material, and forgot important information shortly after learning it. He would start projects with good intentions but frequently put things off until the last minute, resulting in work that didn't reflect his actual capabilities. What it was, what he wasn't doing, and what he needed, he knew. But he needed a little bit of a push.

What bothered Carlos most was that he could see other students in his class who seemed to approach their work more thoughtfully and consistently. Maya, his friend, always seemed calm and prepared, asking great questions during class discussions and turning in work that showed careful consideration. His classmate Alex could explain complex concepts clearly and seemed to remember information from earlier lessons that Carlos had completely forgotten.

"I wish I could think the way they do," Carlos told his older sister Elena that evening. *"Some people are just naturally better at school than others."*

Elena, who was studying to become a teacher, sat down beside him. *"You know, Carlos, I used to think the same thing. I thought some people were just born with better thinking skills, and there wasn't much I could do about it. But then I learned something interesting in my education classes."*

She explained that research had shown that *thinking skills weren't just natural talents* that some people had and others didn't. Like any other skill, like playing the piano or riding a bike, thinking abilities can be developed and improved through *practice and the right kinds of habits.*

"The students who seem naturally good at thinking things through," Elena continued, *"are usually just students who have developed good thinking habits without* realizing *it. They've learned to* **approach problems systematically***, to* **check their work carefully***, and to* **connect new information to things** *they already know."* Elena was explaining something that teachers know is called **stacking**. What's stacking, and how does it work?

Your brain functions similarly to building with blocks since it *needs time to construct new knowledge.* Learning requires us to begin with a single block before we can proceed to place another block on top of it, followed by additional blocks. You can't rush through these processes because doing that leads to the collapse of your work. You have to proceed carefully and build slowly.

Our brains follow the same process as building blocks through the stacking method. Learning new information requires the stacking method because *each new piece must rest on existing knowledge*. It's the reason we have to go slow when we learn the alphabet and any math; it has to be firmly placed in memory before we proceed. .

Reading was the first skill you acquired as you developed your abilities. Learning to interpret squiggles on a page brought you new joy because you discovered meaning in these shapes. You began your reading journey after someone taught you the basic "A" sound to "ahh" pronunciation. After "A" you were taught the "ahh" sound, "B" produced its pronunciation as "buh." The process was probably quite slow until one day when you gained the ability to read the words "cat" and "dog." You then went on to *read sentences, paragraphs, and finally books*. See how learning the alphabet and then building on it to read words is stacking? It was all stacked all the way.

Math learning follows the same pattern as other subjects. You now perform mental addition with no conscious effort to do so. *Learning to count to ten* once seemed like an enormous accomplishment. Even learning your numbers when you were younger was sometimes frustrating. The understanding of basic number counting became necessary before addition could have any meaning. So first learning numbers and then how to use them in addition, subtraction, multiplication, and division. it was all a stacking exercise.

Riding a bike serves as a perfect example in this situation. When you started riding a bike with training wheels, you felt happy about your progress as you cycled in the driveway. The day when training wheels disappeared brought a mix of fear and thrill to your experience.

Your learning process included someone standing behind you (as I said earlier) to hold the seat before you successfully balanced on your own. The experience would have been almost impossible if you had tried your first bike ride without training wheels. The training wheels were part of the stack.

Learning through video games is similar to other educational activities. The first level introduces fundamental moves, which serve as a foundation for progressively harder levels that contain previous knowledge.

This method produces real results because once you master fundamental concepts, new knowledge becomes accessible more quickly. Your brain understands the connection by saying, "*Oh, I get it*" between the new information and your previously learned material. There's another example of how stacking helps kids learn sports. And here we need to think about another concept that is called **muscle memory**.

You know that our brains contain special cells to hold memories. Well, our muscles also can work with the brain and contain memory. However, when discussing muscles, memory refers to the movements and maneuvers involved in sports and other physical activities. Once we keep repeating these physical actions, like we also do in martial arts practice, it becomes a habit, and we move without thinking.

In basketball, you practice shooting five free throws each day after school. Your body needs to learn to remember the movements at first, but after several weeks, it develops a natural expectation for those shots. Your natural progression leads you to shoot ten free throws because five seems too simple, and now your habit develops independently.

The coolest part? Good habits serve as the foundation for developing additional good habits. Brushing teeth becomes automatic, so flossing becomes simpler because you already stand at the sink. what do you have now? A habit tower that functions as a base to construct additional habits in the surrounding area. Believe it or not, learning requires habits. You may have heard that habits are not good things. But here, that's not true. They are essential to learning.

When you feel that learning is difficult or slow, remember that *you are doing something remarkable through gradual progress.*

Carlos understood what Elena was saying and was intrigued but skeptical. "*So you're saying I could become a better thinker just by changing my habits?*" He may not have been seeing it right away, but she was teaching him about stacking. In this case, the habits were the initial learned elements that he would build on, and they would help him become a better, more involved student.

"*Exactly,*" Elena said enthusiastically. "*But here's the key, and it's not about making big changes all at once. It's about **developing small, consistent practices** that gradually become automatic. Just like brushing your teeth or tying your shoes, good thinking can become a habit that you do without even having to think about it.*"

Understanding the Power of Habits

Elena helped Carlos understand that habits were incredibly powerful because they allowed people to perform complex behaviors automatically, without having to use willpower or conscious effort every single time. It was just as though they came naturally after the practice had been started for a while. When something became a habit, it felt natural and simple rather than difficult and exhausting.

Carlos realized that this was exactly what happened with many of his daily routines. He didn't have to think about the steps involved in getting ready for school each morning like showering, brushing his teeth, getting dressed, and eating breakfast; they had all become automatic habits that required very little mental energy.

Elena then explained that the same principle applied to thinking skills. Instead of having to consciously remember to check his work, ask clarifying questions, or connect new information to previous learning, Carlos could develop habits that **made these behaviors automatic and effortless.**

The amazing thing about thinking habits is that once they become automatic, they actually make learning easier and more enjoyable. Instead of feeling like you're constantly struggling to remember what you're supposed to do, good thinking habits free up your mental energy to focus on understanding and enjoying the material you're learning. And always remember that asking good questions is a key part of learning. Never be afraid to ask questions. People who don't ask questions are stopping themselves from learning and understanding.

Designing a Personal Thinking Routine

Inspired by Elena's explanation, Carlos decided to design his own set of thinking habits that could help him become the kind of student he wanted to be. Rather than trying to change everything at once, Elena suggested that he **start by identifying just a few specific areas** where better habits could make the biggest difference.

Carlos thought about the times when his thinking felt scattered and unfocused. He realized that a few patterns emerged from his self-reflection.

Morning Mental Preparation

Carlos noticed that he often started his school day feeling rushed and scattered. He would wake up at the last possible moment, hurry through his morning routine, and arrive at school feeling a bit upset and unprepared for the day. On days when this happened, it was difficult to focus during first period, and he often felt behind for the rest of the day.

Elena suggested that Carlos experiment with **creating a morning routine** that prepared his mind for learning, not just his body for school. This didn't mean waking up hours earlier or doing anything complicated. All he had to do was add a few simple practices that could help him start the day feeling calm and focused.

He decided to try **waking up just fifteen minutes earlier** than usual and using that time for what he called "**morning mental preparation**." During these fifteen minutes, he would **review his schedule** for the day, think about **what he hoped to learn or accomplish**, and **set one specific goal** for himself.

The goal didn't have to be dramatic. It might be **paying extra attention during math class**, or **asking at least one question in science**, or **checking my work carefully** on the history quiz. The important thing was to start each day with a clear intention rather than just letting things happen randomly.

Learning Checkpoints

Carlos also realized that he often went through entire class periods without really monitoring whether he was understanding the material. He would sit in class, listen to the teacher, take some notes, and only discover later, often during homework or a test, that he had missed important concepts. Why didn't he speak up and ask the teacher for more information when he didn't understand? It wasn't that he was lazy; he just **wasn't paying attention.**

Elena suggested that Carlos try building regular **learning checkpoints** into his school day. These were brief moments when he would pause and **ask himself simple questions** about his understanding: *"Do I understand what the teacher just explained?" "Can I think of an example of this concept?" "What questions do I have about this topic?"*

Carlos started setting a goal of having **at least two learning checkpoints** during each class period. He would use moments when the teacher moved from one topic to another, or when they asked if there were questions, as opportunities to check on his own understanding.

If Carlos realized during a checkpoint that he was confused about something, he could *ask a clarifying question right away* rather than discovering the gap in his understanding hours or days later. If he felt confident about the material, the checkpoint served as a moment to reinforce his learning and make connections to previous topics.

End-of-Day Reflection

Finally, Carlos noticed that he often moved from one day to the next without really thinking about what he had learned or what had gone well or poorly. This meant that he kept making the same mistakes repeatedly and missed opportunities to build on his successes.

Elena suggested that Carlos *try ending each school day with a brief reflection routine*. This didn't need to be a lengthy journal entry, just a few minutes of thinking about questions like, "*What did I learn today that was interesting or important*?" or "*What went well with my learning today*?" or maybe "*What could I do differently tomorrow?*" She knew that not only would this help him in his learning efforts, but it would also help him in his self-esteem. Becoming a better student would create a feedback loop that would enhance his self-esteem and prepare him better for future tests.

Carlos decided to combine this reflection time with his after-school snack. While he ate and relaxed, he would spend five minutes thinking about his day and perhaps jotting down a few notes about what he wanted to remember or change.

Starting Small and Building Gradually

Elena emphasized that the key to building sustainable habits was simple. You started with small, achievable changes rather than trying to transform everything at once. Carlos was now beginning to consider his thinking routine ideas, but Elena cautioned him against trying to implement all of them simultaneously.

"*Habit research shows that people are much more successful when they focus on building one new habit at a time,*" Elena explained. "*Once something becomes automatic, which usually takes a few weeks, then you can add another new habit without overwhelming yourself.*" It was a matter of building by small steps, like anything else, and a foundation of habits would begin his new learning process.

Carlos decided to start with just his *morning mental preparation routine*. For the **first two weeks**, his only goal was to **wake up fifteen minutes earlier** and spend that time thinking about his day and setting one learning intention. He wouldn't worry about learning checkpoints or end-of-day reflections until this first habit felt natural and effortless.

At first, waking up earlier felt difficult, and Carlos sometimes forgot to set a learning intention for the day. But Elena had warned him that new habits often felt awkward and required conscious effort at the beginning. "*The goal isn't to be perfect right away,*" she reminded him. "*The goal is to practice the habit consistently enough that it starts to feel natural.*"

After about ten days, Carlos noticed that his morning routine was beginning to feel more automatic. He was waking up at the earlier time without feeling as tired, and he found himself naturally thinking about his learning goals as he got ready for school. More importantly, he noticed that he was arriving at school feeling more focused and prepared for the day ahead.

Adding Learning Checkpoints

Once his morning routine felt established, Carlos began working on incorporating learning checkpoints into his classroom experience. This habit proved more challenging than his morning routine because it required him to remember to pause and self-assess while he was in the middle of following along with class activities.

He experimented with different strategies for remembering to check his understanding. At first, he tried setting specific times, such as every fifteen minutes, but found that this didn't go well with the natural flow of his classes. Then he tried associating checkpoints with specific events, such as whenever the teacher wrote something on the board or whenever a classmate asked a question.

Eventually, Carlos found that the most effective approach was to *use the teacher's own transitions as cues* for **his learning checkpoints**. When Mr. Kim said things like, "*Now let's move on to...*" or "*The next thing I want you to understand is...*" Carlos would take a moment to assess whether he had understood the previous concept before focusing on the new material. If he had any difficulty with it, now was the time to address it with Mr. Kim. No more rushing into the next portion of the class without really understanding what he had just heard.

This approach felt more natural because it fit with the structure of the lessons themselves. Carlos wasn't interrupting his focus to check the time or look for other cues; he was using the teacher's own organizational signals as opportunities for self-reflection.

Within a few weeks, Carlos noticed significant changes in his classroom experience. He was catching misunderstandings much more quickly, which meant he could ask clarifying questions before getting completely lost. He was also retaining information better because the regular checkpoints helped him actively engage with the material rather than passively listening.

Developing End-of-Day Reflection

After his learning checkpoints had become more automatic, Carlos added **the third component** of his thinking routine: **end-of-day reflection**. This habit took longer to establish because it didn't have the same natural cues as his other routines. Morning preparation happened at a specific time, and learning checkpoints were triggered by classroom events, but end-of-day reflection required Carlos to remember to pause and think during the transition from school to home activities. First, it was a little unclear, but he knew that if he stuck to it, he could do it.

Carlos found that **connecting his reflection time to his after-school snack** was effective because eating was already an established habit that happened at roughly the same time each day. As he ate his snack and decompressed from school, he would spend a few minutes thinking about what had gone well, what he had learned, and what he wanted to approach differently the next day.

Initially, Carlos wasn't sure what to focus on during his reflection time. Elena suggested that he start with very simple questions and gradually develop more sophisticated reflection skills. His first week of reflection focused just on identifying one thing he had learned and one thing he was proud of from each school day.

As this basic reflection became more comfortable, Carlos began asking himself more analytical questions. He would think about which of his learning strategies had been most effective that day, what topics he needed to review or get help with, and how he could apply what he had learned to other subjects or situations.

Seeing the Results

After about two months of consistently practicing his thinking routine, Carlos began to notice significant changes in his school performance and his overall learning. The changes weren't dramatic or sudden, but they were steady and meaningful.

Improved Focus and Preparation

The morning mental preparation routine had transformed how he experienced the beginning of each school day. Instead of feeling scattered and reactive, he arrived at school with clear intentions and a sense of purpose. This improved focus carried through into his first-period class and often set a positive tone for the entire day.

His teachers noticed that Carlos seemed more engaged and prepared. Mr. Kim commented that Carlos was asking more thoughtful questions and seemed to be following lessons more actively than he had earlier in the year.

Better Understanding and Retention

The learning checkpoints Carlos had built into his classroom experience were helping him stay connected to the material in real time rather than discovering problems later. He was asking more questions during class, which led to better understanding and fewer moments of confusion during homework and tests.

Carlos also found that he was retaining information much better than before. The regular moments of self-assessment helped him identify what he understood clearly and what needed more attention, leading to more effective studying and review.

More Thoughtful Learning

Perhaps most importantly, Carlos's end-of-day reflection habit was helping him become more intentional and strategic about his learning. Instead of just moving from one assignment to the next without much thought, he was beginning to see patterns in what worked well for him and what didn't.

This metacognitive awareness (thinking about his own thinking) was helping Carlos become more independent and effective as a learner. He was developing a better understanding of his strengths and challenges, which allowed him to adapt his approach to different subjects and assignments.

Sharing the Success

As Carlos's academic performance improved and his confidence grew, his friends noticed the changes. When Maya asked him what he was doing differently, Carlos was excited to share what he had learned about thinking habits.

"I used to think that some people were just naturally better at school," Carlos explained to Maya and their friend Alex during lunch. *"But it turns out that a lot of what I thought was natural talent was actually **just good habits** that people had developed."*

He described his morning preparation, learning checkpoints, and reflection routine, emphasizing that *the key was starting small and building gradually*. Maya was particularly interested in the learning checkpoints idea, because she had struggled with staying focused during longer class periods.

Alex was curious about the reflection routine, wondering if it might help him remember and connect ideas across different subjects. The three friends decided to experiment with adapting Carlos's thinking habits to their own needs and learning styles.

Over the following weeks, they supported each other in developing and maintaining their thinking routines. They would check in during lunch about how their new habits were working and share strategies for overcoming challenges or adapting routines to different situations.

Expanding and Adapting the Routine

As Carlos became more comfortable with his basic thinking routine, he began to experiment with additional habits that could further support his learning and critical thinking development. Elena encouraged this experimentation but reminded him to *add new habits gradually* rather than overwhelming himself.

Reading and Research Habits

Carlos noticed that when he read textbook chapters or researched topics for projects, he often read without really engaging with the material. Elena suggested that he experiment with more active reading habits, such as *pausing periodically to summarize* what he had just read or *asking himself questions* about how new information connected to what he already knew.

Carlos began using a simple strategy he called "**stop and connect**." Every few paragraphs while reading, he would *pause and ask himself two questions*: "**What is the main idea of what I just read?**" and "**How does this connect to something I already know or have experienced?**"

This habit helped Carlos read more thoughtfully and remember information much better. It also made reading more interesting because he was actively looking for connections and patterns rather than just trying to get through the assigned pages.

Problem-Solving Habits

In math class, Carlos had often struggled with word problems because he would rush to calculate without really understanding what the problem was asking. He created a simple problem-solving routine: **first** read the problem **twice**, then **identify the given information** and the **question being asked**, then consider what strategy or formula might be helpful, and finally solve the problem step by step while checking his work along the way.

This systematic approach dramatically improved Carlos's performance on math assignments and tests. More importantly, *it reduced his anxiety about math* because he had a reliable process to follow rather than just hoping he would figure out what to do. If he had a problem there was no difficulty in asking the teacher to explain it again until he understood.

Social and Collaborative Habits

Carlos also began developing habits that improved his collaboration and communication with classmates. He noticed that during group projects, he sometimes dominated conversations or, conversely, stayed too quiet and didn't contribute his ideas effectively.

Elena suggested that Carlos practice the **habits of active listening** and thoughtful contribution during group work. This meant paying attention to what others were saying, **asking clarifying questions** when he didn't understand someone's idea, and **sharing his own thoughts** in ways that built on the group's discussion rather than just stating his opinion.

These social thinking habits helped Carlos become a more effective team member and also improved his understanding of different perspectives on complex topics.

The Ripple Effect

As Carlos's thinking habits became more established and automatic, he began to notice that they were influencing areas of his life beyond academics. The skills he was developing for monitoring his understanding, reflecting on his experiences, and approaching problems systematically were proving useful in many different ways.

When Carlos had disagreements with friends or family members, he found himself naturally pausing to consider different perspectives and asking clarifying questions rather than just reacting emotionally. When he faced decisions about how to spend his free time or which activities to pursue, he was more thoughtful about considering his goals and values.

The confidence Carlos gained from improving his academic performance also carried over into other areas. He felt more willing to try new activities, take on leadership roles, and speak up in group discussions because he had *developed trust in his own thinking abilities.*

Elena pointed out that the ripple effect was one of the most valuable aspects of developing good thinking habits. *"When you improve your ability to think clearly and learn effectively,"* she explained, *"those skills benefit every area of your life, not just school."*

Building Your Own Thinking Day

Carlos's experience showed that developing better thinking habits was possible for anyone willing to start small and be consistent. The specific habits that worked best for Carlos might not be identical to what would work for other students, but the principles stretched to all parts of his life.

Start with Self-Assessment

Before developing new habits, it's helpful to honestly assess your current thinking patterns. When do you feel most focused and effective? When do you struggle with understanding or remembering information? What kind of mistakes do you make repeatedly? Understanding your current patterns helps you identify which new habits would be most beneficial.

Choose One Habit to Begin

Rather than trying to change multiple behaviors at once, focus on building one new thinking habit at a time. Choose something that feels achievable and important, and decide to practice it consistently for at least two to three weeks before adding anything else.

Connect New Habits to Existing Routines

New habits are easier to establish when they're connected to things you already do regularly. Carlos connected his morning thinking time to his existing wake-up routine, his learning checkpoints to classroom transitions, and his reflection time to his after-school snack.

Be Patient with the Process

Building habits takes time and consistent practice. Don't expect new behaviors to feel natural immediately, and don't give up if you forget or struggle at first. The goal is gradual improvement, not immediate perfection.

Adapt and Experiment

As your habits become more established, you can experiment with modifications and additions that better suit your learning style and goals. What works for one person might need to be adapted for another person's schedule, preferences, or challenges.

Chapter Summary

Carlos's journey from scattered, reactive learning to developing consistent thinking habits demonstrates that critical thinking skills can be cultivated through daily practices and routines. By starting with small, achievable changes and building habits gradually, Carlos transformed his morning preparation, classroom engagement, and reflection practices. The key principles include starting with self-assessment, focusing on one habit at a time, connecting new behaviors to existing routines, being patient with the development process, and adapting habits to personal needs and circumstances. Most importantly, Carlos discovered thinking habits create a ripple effect that benefits not just academic performance but all areas of life, building confidence and competence that extend far beyond the classroom.

Chapter 9: Seeing Things Differently

Mia Thompson stood in front of her easel in the school art room, fighting back tears of frustration. What was supposed to be a beautiful landscape painting for the spring art show had turned into what she considered a complete disaster. The assignment had been straightforward: paint a scene from nature that showed depth and perspective using the techniques they had been practicing all semester. It had seemed simple enough initially, but now she felt she had failed.

Mia had painted the view from her bedroom window, which looked out over a small pond surrounded by willow trees. In her mind, she could see exactly how the painting should look: the graceful trees reflected in the still water, the soft morning light filtering through the branches, and the peaceful mood of early spring. She had been excited about capturing this beautiful scene that she saw every morning when she woke up.

But nothing had gone according to plan. When Mia tried to paint the willow branches, they looked stiff and unnatural instead of flowing and graceful. The reflection in the water became a muddy mess when she tried to blend the colors. The perspective looked all wrong. The trees seemed to be floating in the air rather than growing from the ground, and the pond looked more like a blue blob than a body of water.

To make matters worse, Mia had accidentally knocked over her water jar halfway through the painting session, sending dirty water cascading across her canvas. Instead of the soft, dreamy landscape she had envisioned, her painting now featured strange drips and splotches that seemed to have minds of their own.

"*This is terrible,*" Mia whispered to herself, staring at the canvas with dismay. "*Everyone else's paintings look so much better than mine. Mrs. Garcia is going to think I didn't even try.*"

Her friend Sofia, who was working on her own painting at the next easel, glanced over with concern. "*What's wrong, Mia? You look really upset.*"

Mia gestured helplessly at her painting. "*Look at this mess! It's supposed to be a peaceful pond with willow trees, but it looks like... I don't even know what it looks like. It's just a disaster.*"

Sofia studied Mia's canvas for a moment, tilting her head to one side. "*You know,*" she said thoughtfully, "*it doesn't look like a disaster to me. It actually looks kind of... mysterious and magical.*"

Mia blinked in surprise. "*What do you mean?*"

"*Well,*" Sofia continued, pointing to different areas of the painting, "*these drips and splotches that you think are mistakes actually look like rain falling, or maybe like the trees are crying happy tears. And this part where the colors got all mixed together looks like morning mist rising from the water. It's really atmospheric and dreamlike.*"

Mia looked at her painting again, trying to see what Sofia was describing. She had been so focused on how different her painting was from what she had originally planned that she hadn't considered whether it might have its own unique beauty.

When Mrs. Garcia Surprised Everyone

When art class ended, Mrs. Garcia walked around the room to look at each student's work in progress. Mia watched nervously as the teacher approached her easel, preparing herself for disappointment or gentle suggestions about how to fix her obvious mistakes.

Mrs. Garcia stopped in front of Mia's painting and stood quietly for a long moment, studying the canvas with the same serious attention she gave to all the artwork in their classroom. Mia held her breath, waiting for the critique she was certain was coming.

"*Mia,*" Mrs. Garcia said finally, "t*his is absolutely fascinating. Can you tell me about your creative process here?*"

Mia's eyes widened in confusion. "*My creative process? But... it's not what it's supposed to be. I was trying to paint a realistic landscape, and everything went wrong. The water spilled, and the colors got all muddy, and nothing looks the way I planned.*"

Mrs. Garcia smiled warmly. "*Sometimes the most interesting art happens when we let go of our original plans and allow the painting to become something unexpected. What you've created here has a wonderful sense of movement and emotion that many realistic paintings lack.*"

She pointed to the areas where the spilled water had created irregular drips and streaks. "*These vertical elements create a sense of rain or falling water that adds drama to the scene. And the way the colors have blended here in the center gives the painting a dreamlike quality that draws the viewer in.*"

Mia stared at her teacher in amazement. "*You really think it's good?*"

"I think it's unique and expressive," Mrs. Garcia replied. "Not every painting needs to look exactly like a photograph of the real world. Some of the most powerful artwork throughout history has been created by artists who saw familiar subjects in completely new ways."

Mrs. Garcia called the rest of the class over to look at Mia's painting. *"I want everyone to see this excellent example of how happy accidents can become artistic innovations. Mia has created something that's much more interesting than a standard landscape because she was willing to embrace the unexpected."*

As her classmates gathered around, Mia felt a mix of pride and bewilderment. Just minutes earlier, she had been convinced that her painting was a failure. Now her teacher was using it as an example of creative innovation, and her friends were commenting on aspects of the work that they found beautiful and engaging.

Learning to Reframe Perspective

After class, Mrs. Garcia asked Mia to stay for a few minutes to talk about what had happened during the painting session. *"I can see that you were initially upset about your painting,"* she said. *"Can you help me understand what you were feeling?"*

Mia explained how she had started the day with a clear vision of what she wanted to create and how frustrated she had become when nothing turned out the way she had planned. *"I kept comparing my painting to what I had imagined, and it seemed like a complete failure,"* she said.

Mrs. Garcia nodded understandingly. *"That's a very natural reaction, and it's something that happens to professional artists all the time. But here's something important that I've learned over many years of making and teaching art: there's almost always more than one way to look at any situation."*

She explained that Mia had been viewing her painting through what she called a "**comparison lens**"—judging it based on how closely it matched her original intention. But there were other lenses through which the same painting could be viewed.

"When I looked at your painting," Mrs. Garcia continued, *"I was using what we might call an '**exploration lens**.' Instead of asking whether your painting matched a predetermined idea, I was asking what unique qualities and emotions your painting expressed on its own terms."*

Mrs. Garcia helped Mia understand that the principle of multiple perspectives applied to much more than just artwork. In almost any situation, there were different ways to interpret what was happening, different aspects to focus on, and different criteria for evaluating success or failure.

"Learning to shift perspectives isn't about lying to yourself or pretending that problems don't exist," Mrs. Garcia explained. *"It's about developing the flexibility to see situations from multiple angles so that you can respond more thoughtfully and creatively."*

Discovering Hidden Strengths

Over the following days, Mia found herself thinking frequently about Mrs. Garcia's comments about perspective and reframing. She began to notice how often she automatically interpreted situations in ways that made her feel frustrated or inadequate, without considering whether there might be other equally valid ways to understand what was happening.

For example, Mia had always considered herself a slow reader compared to her friend Jake, who could finish novels in just a few days. This comparison had made her feel self-conscious about her reading abilities and reluctant to take part in book discussions with her friends.

But when Mia applied Mrs. Garcia's perspective-shifting approach to her reading habits, she realized that she noticed details and nuances in stories that Jake often missed. While Jake read quickly for plot and excitement, Mia read more slowly because she was naturally paying attention to character development, descriptive language, and thematic elements.

Instead of viewing her reading speed as a weakness, Mia began to appreciate it as a different kind of strength. She wasn't a slow reader; she was a thorough reader who engaged deeply with literature. This realization gave her the confidence to share her insights during book discussions, where her thoughtful observations were welcomed and valued by her friends and teachers.

The Butterfly Effect of New Perspectives

As Mia became more skilled at shifting perspectives, she noticed that this ability was creating positive changes in many areas of her life. Situations that had previously caused her stress or disappointment became opportunities for creative problem-solving and personal growth.

Academic Challenges

When Mia struggled with a particularly difficult math unit on fractions, her first instinct was to feel frustrated and assume that she was "bad at math." But remembering Mrs. Garcia's lesson about multiple perspectives, Mia tried reframing the situation.

Instead of viewing her confusion as a sign of inadequacy, Mia began to see it as useful information about which concepts needed more attention. Rather than comparing herself to classmates who seemed to understand fractions easily, Mia focused on her own progress and the specific strategies that helped her learn most effectively.

This perspective shift transformed Mia's relationship with challenging academic material. Instead of avoiding difficult subjects or giving up quickly when she encountered confusion, Mia developed the habit of asking herself, *"What can this challenge teach me?"* and *"How might this difficulty actually be helping me become a better learner?"*

Social Situations

Mia also applied perspective-shifting to her social relationships. When her friend group went through a period of tension and disagreement, Mia's initial reaction was to worry that their friendships were falling apart and that she was somehow responsible for the conflict.

But using her new perspective skills, Mia considered other ways to interpret the situation. Perhaps the tension was a sign that her friends felt safe enough with each other to express their honest opinions. Maybe the disagreement was an opportunity for them to understand each other better and develop stronger communication skills.

This reframing helped Mia approach the situation more calmly and constructively. Instead of withdrawing from her friends or trying to avoid conflict entirely, Mia was able to listen thoughtfully to different viewpoints and help her friend group work through their disagreements in a way that ultimately strengthened their relationships.

Family Dynamics

At home, Mia's new perspective skills helped her navigate the sometimes frustrating experience of living with her energetic younger brother Danny. Danny had a habit of interrupting Mia's homework time with requests for help, questions about her activities, and invitations to play games.

Previously, Mia had viewed these interruptions primarily as annoyances that interfered with her productivity. But when she tried looking at the situation from Danny's perspective, she realized that his interruptions were actually expressions of admiration and a desire to spend time with his big sister.

This realization didn't mean that Mia never needed focused study time, but it did help her respond to Danny with more patience and creativity. She began setting aside specific times when Danny could have her full attention, which satisfied his need for connection while protecting her need for concentrated work.

The Art Show Revelation

When the spring art show arrived, Mia felt nervous but excited about displaying her painting. She had continued working on it after that first transformative class session, building on the unexpected effects that had initially seemed like disasters.

The painting that resulted from this process was unlike anything else in the show. While many of her classmates had created technically proficient realistic landscapes, Mia's painting had an emotional and atmospheric quality that drew viewers in and invited them to interpret the scene in their own ways.

During the art show opening, Mia was amazed by the variety of responses her painting received. Some viewers saw a rainstorm passing over a peaceful pond. Others interpreted the drips and flowing colors as representing the cycle of water in nature. Several people commented on the sense of movement and life in the painting, noting that it seemed to capture the dynamic energy of the natural world rather than just its static appearance.

After carefully looking at Mia's painting, an older woman smiled and approached her. *"This painting reminds me of a poem by Emily Dickinson about rain and renewal,"* she said. *"There's something about the way you've captured the interaction between water and earth that feels very spiritual and hopeful."*

Mia was moved by this response and by the realization that her painting was communicating emotions and ideas that she hadn't consciously intended to express. The "mistakes" that had initially distressed her had become the most powerful and meaningful elements of the artwork.

Teaching Others to Shift Perspectives

Inspired by her own transformation, Mia began looking for opportunities to help others discover the power of perspective-shifting. When her friend Marcus was disappointed about not making the school soccer team, Mia helped him consider alternative ways to interpret the situation.

Instead of viewing the rejection as a sign that he wasn't good enough for organized sports, Marcus began to see it as an opportunity to explore other activities that might be even better suited to his interests and talents. He ended up joining the school's hiking club, where he discovered a passion for outdoor exploration and environmental conservation that ultimately became a major focus of his high school and college years.

When her little brother Danny was upset about a project that didn't turn out the way he had planned, Mia shared some of the perspective-shifting techniques she had learned from Mrs. Garcia. Together, they looked for unexpected positive aspects of Danny's project and brainstormed ways to build on what he had created rather than starting over.

Mia also began incorporating perspective-shifting into her approach to group projects and collaborative work at school. When team members disagreed about directions or approaches, Mia would suggest that they take time to understand each person's viewpoint before trying to reach a consensus. This practice often revealed creative solutions that no one had initially considered.

The Science of Perspective

Curious about the psychology behind perspective-shifting, Mia decided to research the topic for a science project. She learned that the ability to see situations from multiple viewpoints was connected to several important cognitive and emotional skills.

Cognitive Flexibility

Mia discovered that perspective-shifting was related to something called cognitive flexibility, the mental ability to switch between different concepts or to think about multiple concepts simultaneously. This skill was crucial for creative problem-solving, adaptability, and learning from experience.

Research showed that people with higher cognitive flexibility were better at finding innovative solutions to problems, adapting to new situations, and recovering from setbacks. They were also more likely to see opportunities in challenging circumstances and to maintain emotional equilibrium during times of change or stress.

Emotional Regulation

Mia also learned that perspective-shifting was a powerful tool for emotional regulation. When people could view situations from multiple angles, they were less likely to become overwhelmed by negative emotions and more likely to maintain hope and motivation during difficult times.

This didn't mean that perspective-shifting involved denying or minimizing genuine problems. Rather, it provided a more complete and different understanding of complex situations, which often revealed resources, opportunities, and solutions that weren't visible from a single viewpoint.

Empathy and Social Understanding

Perhaps most importantly, Mia discovered that perspective-shifting was fundamental to empathy and healthy social relationships. The ability to understand how situations looked from other people's viewpoints was essential for effective communication, conflict resolution, and collaborative problem-solving.

People who were skilled at perspective-shifting were better at understanding why others behaved the way they did, even when those behaviors initially seemed confusing or unreasonable. This understanding led to more compassionate and effective responses to interpersonal challenges.

Building Perspective-Shifting Skills

Through her research and personal experience, Mia identified several strategies that could help anyone develop stronger perspective-shifting abilities.

The Multiple Lens Technique

Mia learned to approach complex situations by consciously trying on different "lenses" or frameworks for interpretation. For example, when facing a challenge, she might look at it through a *"learning lens"* (**what can this teach me**?), a *"growth lens"* (**how might this help me develop new skills**?), or a *"connection lens"* (**how might this bring me closer to others**?).

The Other Person's Shoes Method

When interpersonal conflicts or misunderstandings arose, Mia practiced imagining how the situation looked from the other person's perspective. What pressures might they be facing? What goals or values might be motivating their behavior? What fears or concerns might be influencing their reactions?

The Time Travel Approach

Mia also found it helpful to consider how current challenges might look from different points in time. How would she view this situation a week from now? A year from now? How might her future self advise her current self to respond?

The Possibility Expansion Exercise

When faced with situations that seemed to have limited options, Mia would challenge herself to brainstorm as many alternative interpretations and responses as possible, even ones that initially seemed silly or unrealistic. This exercise often revealed creative possibilities that she hadn't initially considered.

The Ripple Effects Continue

As Mia's perspective-shifting skills became more developed and automatic, she noticed that they were influencing not just her own life but also the lives of people around her. Friends and family members began coming to her for advice when they were feeling stuck or overwhelmed by challenging situations.

Mia's reputation as someone who could help others see new possibilities and creative solutions grew among her classmates and teachers. She was often asked to participate in peer mediation when conflicts arose, and her teachers noticed her ability to help classmates work through creative blocks and academic challenges.

Most importantly, Mia's experience had taught her that resilience and creativity weren't just natural talents that some people possessed and others lacked. They were *skills that could be developed through practice* and the conscious cultivation of mental flexibility.

Creating a Culture of Multiple Perspectives

Inspired by the positive changes in her own life and relationships, Mia began advocating for perspective-shifting practices in various contexts. She suggested that her art class begin critiques by having students identify multiple positive qualities in each artwork before discussing areas for improvement.

She proposed that her social studies class examine historical events from the viewpoints of different groups of people, rather than just learning a single official narrative. She even convinced her family to try a weekly dinner conversation where they would discuss current events or family decisions from multiple perspectives before reaching conclusions.

These practices created environments where creativity, empathy, and innovative thinking flourished. Problems that had seemed intractable became opportunities for collaborative problem-solving.

Conflicts that had seemed irreconcilable became chances to develop deeper understanding and stronger relationships.

A New Definition of Success

Perhaps the most profound change in Mia's thinking *involved her understanding of success and failure*. Before learning about perspective-shifting, Mia had viewed these as fixed, objective categories. Something either succeeded or failed based on predetermined criteria, and there wasn't much room for alternative interpretations.

But her experience with the art project and subsequent practice with perspective-shifting had taught her that success and failure were often matters of interpretation and framing. What looked like failure from one perspective might be valuable learning, a creative breakthrough, or an unexpected opportunity from another viewpoint.

This didn't mean that Mia became careless about goals or indifferent to outcomes. Rather, she developed a more sophisticated understanding of how to evaluate experiences and a greater capacity to find value and meaning in all kinds of situations.

Mia learned to ask not just "*Did this turn out the way I planned*?" but also "*What did I learn from this experience*?" and "*How did this challenge help me grow*?" or "*What unexpected opportunities did this situation create*?" and "*How can I use what happened to help others or to approach future challenges more effectively*?"

Chapter Summary

Mia's journey from viewing her "failed" art project as a disaster to recognizing it as a creative breakthrough illustrates the **transformative power of perspective-shifting.** By learning to view situations through multiple lenses rather than just one predetermined framework, Mia discovered hidden strengths, found creative solutions to problems, and developed greater resilience and empathy. The ability to shift perspectives is a learnable skill that involves cognitive flexibility, emotional regulation, and social understanding. Key strategies include trying on different interpretive lenses, imagining other people's viewpoints, considering how situations might look from different points in time, and expanding the range of possible responses to challenges. Most important, perspective-shifting reveals that success and failure are often matters of interpretation, and that almost any experience can become a source of learning, growth, and creative opportunity when viewed from the right angle.

Chapter 10: Stress and Your Thinking Brain

Kevin Liu sat before his math test while his heart thundered so loudly it seemed everyone in the entire classroom could hear it. He was upset. During his homework practice the night before, all the numbers and equations had looked perfectly clear, but now they seemed like unknown writing on an invisible page. He didn't understand because it had seemed so clear before, and now it was all a muddle. The combination of his sweaty hands and stomach turmoil and chest tightness caused his breathing to be more difficult. What was happening? He felt like he couldn't do it.

The unit test about fractions, which Mr. Rodriguez had taught the class for three weeks, was right in front of him. Kevin had studied his material thoroughly and finished all his homework, even adding extra practice problems to confirm his understanding of the subject. He had solved identical problems with ease during the previous day. But now he felt lost. He sat in the quiet classroom with the test sheet in front of him, but his brain seemed to have stopped working completely.

The initial problem required him to combine two fractions that had different denominators. Kevin followed the right procedure by locating a common denominator to convert both fractions, then adding their numerators and simplifying when appropriate. But while attempting to solve the problem, he made careless errors and doubted his abilities. His thinking became disorganized as his mind produced anxious thoughts that stopped him from following the correct instructions.

Anxiety was going to cause him to fail this test, and he knew it, but he was having trouble calming himself down. . He worried about his mathematics skills because he believed he wasn't good enough. *"What if my parents are disappointed? What if I don't understand fractions as well as everyone else in the class?"*

Kevin's worrying made him lose focus on the actual mathematical work. He spent multiple attempts reading the same question, yet failed to get its meaning. Basic operations that normally required no effort became extremely challenging, and he constantly lost his place during multi-step calculations. The more he tried, the worse it seemed to get. He was in the grip of anxiety, but he didn't really understand what was happening.

The first twenty minutes of the fifty-minute test period passed, and Kevin managed to solve only three out of fifteen questions without feeling certain about his solutions. Panic overtook him as he watched other kids steadily working on their tests while he was frozen by fear. Other kids were finishing their tests and placing them on the teacher's table, while he sat here unable to think about problems he easily solved last night.

Kevin raised his hand tentatively. Mr. Rodriguez approached Kevin's desk, where he whispered about his inability to think clearly. *"The problems should be straightforward for me, but my brain* is functioning *abnormally right now."*

Mr. Rodriguez's Understanding Response

During his fifteen years of teaching experience, Mr. Rodriguez had seen this exact situation multiple times. He identified test anxiety because Kevin clearly showed the typical symptoms of stress.

Mr. Rodriguez leaned down to speak with Kevin at his desk while keeping his voice low. *"Your thinking brain seems to be struggling because of stress response symptoms. A lot of kids face this situation, and there are some basic things that help reduce stress while helping with mental clarity."*

Kevin's gaze met Mr. Rodriguez's with a blend of hope and puzzlement. *"My stress response? What do you mean?"* This was something new to him.

It was now Mr. Rodriguez's turn to help clear something up for Kevin. In simple terms, he explained that everybody's brain has a natural defense system that sees threats, including test challenges, which leads to the **fight-or-flight response action**. All of us used this survival system successfully to escape predators, yet it proved useless in math testing situations. We didn't have dinosaurs running after us anymore, but testing was feeling just as dangerous. How could that be, and what could Kevin do about it?

Mr. Rodriguez explained to Kevin that *"Your brain sends most of your energy and attention to your body's running and fighting parts when it identifies danger. In fact, your body is telling you to run for your life. Are math tests a reason to feel like your life is in danger?"*

The explanation Kevin got about his situation really helped him. Through this explanation, he gained a better understanding of his physical distress affecting his mental disorganization. Kevin gained a new understanding that he hadn't lost his math abilities. *"My brain has reacted as if I were in danger even though I am safe. What a relief. "*

Mr. Rodriguez confirmed his words. The brain performs its functions, but it requires assistance to understand that this situation requires effort rather than being seen as a threat. Are there any methods you would like to learn that improve mental functioning? I'll bet there are.

Mr. Rodriguez told Kevin to step outside the classroom for a few minutes to learn basic methods for controlling his nervous system.

He provided Kevin with a **specific breathing exercise** that would help his brain recognize safety and relaxation. The hallway offered them space to speak without disturbing other students, so Mr. Rodriguez demonstrated the breathing techniques for brain relaxation. It was that simple?

The breathing exercises, according to Mr. Rodriguez, are a direct link to the nervous system. Your brain receives *signals of safety through deep breathing* because it *enables the transition from emergency response to learning mode.*

Kevin learned the basic *"box breathing" method* that Mr. Rodriguez demonstrated. The steps were *simply breathing in for four counts,* followed by *four counts of holding your breath,* then *four counts of exhaling* before *emptying your lungs for four counts* before beginning another cycle. The process resembles drawing a square through breathing motions, according to Mr. Rodriguez. Anyone could do it, and they could *do it anywhere, at any time* they felt stressed.

At first, Kevin had a bit of trouble following the breathing pattern as his thoughts constantly returned to test-related anxiety. When this happened, Mr. Rodriguez advised him to *refocus on his breath* whenever his thoughts drifted.

The practice of focused breathing enabled Kevin to experience a meaningful change in his mental state within a few minutes. His heart rate reduced while his chest tension decreased, and his thinking patterns became more structured and organized. Although the intense anxiety remained present, it had become more manageable while reducing its intensity.

"*How do you feel now?*" Mr. Rodriguez asked.

Kevin thought about his body before answering. "*Better,*" he said with some surprise.

"*That's perfect,*" Mr. Rodriguez said with a smile. "*You'll probably experience some level of nervousness, which is normal because it demonstrates your commitment to achieving success. Your thinking capabilities should function better with those feelings rather than being overwhelmed by them.*"

The Test Required His New Strategies.

Kevin entered the classroom with a distinct change after his short absence. The test problems kept appearing difficult, but they no longer appeared beyond reach or beyond his understanding. His brain processed mathematical concepts and procedures with improved clarity as his thoughts organized better and became more focused.

Before beginning his test questions, Kevin used his new *breathing method while sitting at his desk.* Three rounds of box breathing brought him to a state of mental clarity that improved his ability to solve math problems with purpose rather than panic.

During his review of the first fraction addition problem with different denominators, Kevin successfully retrieved his knowledge to follow the steps methodically. He determined the common denominator, then transformed the fractions to equivalent ones before adding their numerators and simplifying the outcome. His thinking process became more structured than chaotic despite the difficulty of the task since he continued to concentrate and make a good effort.

While working on these problems, Kevin realized that he could regain his focus by *taking deep breaths whenever anxiety came up*. The breathing method did not simplify his math tasks, but it enabled him to keep his knowledge and problem-solving skills available throughout the entire test.

Kevin learned that *approaching the test with a peaceful state of mind* helped him avoid errors in his responses. His previous anxiety had caused him to speed through problems while repeatedly doubting his answers. Working at his pace allowed him to carefully verify his answers, while he relied on his math logic.

After he finished all fifteen test problems, he had an average level of confidence in his answers. Through this experience, Kevin gained an important technique for stress management, which helped him in all his tests.

Understanding the Science Behind Stress and Thinking

After class, Kevin approached Mr. Rodriguez to ask more questions about test performance because he remained curious about the link between stress and thinking. Mr. Rodriguez was pleased with Kevin's curiosity and spent time explaining the scientific aspects of stress and thinking processes.

The Two-Brain System

According to Mr. Rodriguez, the brain functions as two interconnected systems that sometimes fight against each other. People can identify this first brain system as *both their emotional brain and survival brain* because it *operates rapidly* while providing automatic safety responses. The *"thinking brain"* along with its alternate name *"rational brain"* operates at a slower pace with deliberate actions to solve complex problems. No, we don't have two brains, but the brain does have two systems.

The two brain systems possess distinct roles according to Mr. Rodriguez because *they function independently* while maintaining separate abilities. Your emotional brain functions superbly at *warning you about dangers* while simultaneously getting your body ready for immediate reaction. Your *thinking brain* demonstrates the ability to process complex information and *plan ahead and solve problems* that need multiple steps. One tells you to run while the other wants you to think about it and problem-solve. Both work on your behalf.

During his test anxiety episode, Kevin's emotional brain identified the challenging test as danger, so it triggered his stress response. The activation of stress response shifted his mental resources from his thinking brain, so he struggled to access both his mathematical knowledge and reasoning capabilities.

The Stress Response in Action

Mr. Rodriguez explained to Kevin how the stress response affected his body and brain through multiple physical and mental changes which served to protect him from threats. His heart rate increased for better muscle blood circulation as his breathing became fast and shallow for immediate oxygen supply while stress hormones, entered his bloodstream to deliver emergency energy. It was firing him up to run to safety.

According to Mr. Rodriguez, the complete set of physical changes proves beneficial for escaping dangerous animals yet creates difficulties when someone needs to remain seated and think carefully about mathematical problems.

"The experience was so sudden that I forgot how to solve problems I had mastered the day before," Kevin explained with gratitude. *"The stress*

created a barrier that prevented me from accessing my stored knowledge about mathematics."

The Power of Breathing and Relaxation

How did the breathing exercises help his mental clarity? The nervous system consists of two branches: **the sympathetic nervous system** which **triggers stress** response and the **parasympathetic nervous system** which **enables relaxation and recovery**.

Mr. Rodriguez told Kevin that *breathing slowly while deeply inhaling stimulates the parasympathetic nervous system* to send signals that notify the brain that it can relax. This enables your thinking brain to function properly and return to its normal operation.

Building a Personal Stress Management Toolkit

Kevin started learning additional stress management approaches after having success with breathing exercises in challenging situations. He spent several weeks with Mr. Rodriguez and his school counselor, Ms. Patel, as well as his parents, to build a collection of stress management strategies.

Physical Techniques

Exercise also is a good way to handle stress. Through physical exercises, Kevin acquired several methods to transform from stressed to a focused learning state. Besides *box breathing*, he practiced *progressive muscle relaxation*, where he *tensed different muscle groups* in his body *before relaxing them*. Through this exercise, he gained better awareness of physical tension while learning how to let it go.

Gentle physical movement proved to be an effective approach for stress reduction, according to Kevin. A *brief walk or stretching exercises* or simply standing up for one minute helped his nervous system recover, which improved his concentration.

Mental Techniques

Kevin got additional training now about mental approaches, which help him handle stressful thoughts and stay focused during difficult moments. Ms. Patel showed him how to detect the worrisome thoughts that worsened his stress so he could *swap them with more constructive and realistic thoughts.*

The thought: *"What if I fail this test and everyone thinks I'm stupid?"* Kevin developed a new thought process, which stated, *"The test is difficult yet I've prepared well, and breathing techniques will help me stay composed and focused."*

Next, Kevin trained himself to *use positive self-talk* by using words that supportive friends and teachers would use. Instead of self-criticism for his nervousness, Kevin would accept normal nervousness while remembering his skills and abilities.

Whenever he felt stressed or anxious, Kevin now had multiple ways to help himself, and each of them was working to his benefit.

Environmental Strategies

Even the environment can cause stress, and Kevin was getting help here, too. Ms. Patel worked with Kevin to recognize how *different environmental elements affected his stress levels.* The environment at home received attention from him so he could establish spaces that combined organization with calmness to improve focus and relaxation. His pre-test routine strengthened to provide him with confidence and preparation rather than causing anxiety and confusion.

The *regular routine* before challenging times allowed Kevin's brain to establish patterns, which increased his sense of control. Before each test, Kevin *reviewed his notes briefly* while *practicing deep breathing* to prepare himself using his stress management tools.

Sharing the Knowledge with Others

Kevin noticed his classmates and friends dealing with the same stress management issues after he developed his own stress management abilities. And he wanted to share. Many students faced test anxiety and performance pressure and overwhelming feelings that blocked their ability to demonstrate their actual knowledge and capabilities. He knew what it felt like, and he didn't want to feel that way again. He wanted to help his classmates so that they would feel okay, like him.

Kevin began to teach his friends about the breathing techniques and stress management strategies that proved useful for him. He explained to his friends that these strategies *served more than grade improvement* purposes because they helped people preserve their mental and emotional health.

Helping His Study Group

The students in Kevin's study group adopted stress management techniques as part of their practice. During periods of difficult material stress, the students united to practice breathing breaks or execute brief stress-relief exercises before resuming their work.

The students were now in a supportive learning environment because they could express their difficulties and get assistance from their peers. Group members replaced pretending with perfect understanding by *openly discussing their challenges* to discover collaborative solutions.

Supporting Classmates During Tests

Kevin discovered multiple methods to assist his classmates throughout their actual testing periods. Right before crucial tests, he would discreetly teach breathing exercises to students who demonstrated excessive nervousness. He created unobtrusive hand gestures to alert his friends about deep breathing when they started showing signs of pressure during exams.

The peer-based strategies established a classroom atmosphere that viewed stress management as fundamental for success rather than a weakness.

The Broader Benefits of Stress Management

The stress management skills Kevin mastered led him to realize their value extended past his test results. His ability to remain composed under high-pressure situations proved beneficial in multiple aspects of his daily life.

Sports and Physical Activities

Kevin enjoyed playing basketball, but his performance anxiety during games frequently interfered with his play, especially when the score was tight or when he needed to make critical shots. The mental strategies that Kevin learned for academic situations proved equally effective in basketball games.

Through learning to manage his nervous energy and stay focused during stressful situations, Kevin developed into a more consistent and confident basketball player. The strategic thinking ability of Kevin improved, so he made superior choices regardless of the game's pressure.

Social Situations and Relationships

Stress management skills taught by Kevin brought him better social relationships with his peers. In conflicts with friends and family, he kept a peaceful demeanor, avoiding emotional reactions or defensiveness.

Taking deep breaths while using his thinking brain during conflicts allowed Kevin to express himself better and understand other viewpoints more deeply, which led to innovative solutions for relationship conflicts.

Creative and Artistic Activities

The most unexpected discovery Kevin made was that stress management techniques improved both his creative abilities and his enjoyment of artistic pursuits. He found more willingness to take risks and express himself authentically when he started creative projects from a place of calm relaxation.

Kevin frequently experienced test anxiety about both his creative abilities and how others would judge his work. Through stress management, he learned to experience pleasure from creative expression rather than worrying about criticism or comparing himself to others.

Teaching Stress Management to Younger Students

Ms. Patel recognized Kevin's expertise in stress management, so she asked him to instruct young students who faced their initial standardized tests. The chance to teach others about his learned skills brought Kevin great enthusiasm since he wanted to prevent students from facing his past overwhelming test anxiety.

Third and fourth graders proved more receptive to stress management methods than their older counterparts, according to Kevin. These younger students felt no discomfort about performing breathing exercises and freely shared their emotions and concerns.

Kevin created educational materials that explained the relationship of stress to thinking at a level suitable for his audience. Through simple comparisons, he explained that a stressed brain functions like a computer overloaded with programs, and worried thoughts function like sun-blocking clouds.

Creating Visual Tools

Kevin joined Ms. Patel to develop educational tools that helped younger students understand and practice stress management techniques. Students developed a "calm down toolbox" poster that displayed various relaxation methods, including breathing techniques with gentle body movements and positive self-talk and help requests.

Students developed a basic chart to help them identify their body's stress indicators, which included a quick heart rate, shallow breaths, tight muscles and stomach butterflies. Students learned to identify stress signs in their bodies so they could use their management tools before their anxiety reached critical levels.

Building School-Wide Awareness

The stress management and emotional regulation skills program Kevin started with young students expanded into a schoolwide initiative. Teachers included short relaxation exercises in their regular lessons, and the school counseling office produced materials that parents could use at home to teach stress management techniques.

The entire school approach established emotional regulation as an important value, and students received support to learn these skills for academic success and personal well-being.

The Long-Term Impact

Kevin regarded the overwhelming test day as his life's turning point because he acquired essential life skills instead of focusing on his math test results. The stress management techniques he learned during fifth grade proved useful during all his subsequent academic years and professional career.

He discovered that challenging emotions don't need to prevent clear thinking. And he discovered that proper tools and techniques allowed him to experience difficult emotions while keeping his knowledge and problem-solving capabilities accessible.

Building Your Own Calm Down Toolkit

The ability to manage stress develops into a skill that improves academic success and general health, according to Kevin's experience. Creating your stress management system requires you to try multiple methods until you discover the methods that suit your specific requirements.

Quick Reset Techniques

Each stress management toolkit needs to include fast and unobtrusive methods for handling stressful events. The techniques of deep breathing exercises and progressive muscle relaxation and positive self-talk allow students to use them during testing situations without drawing attention and without using much time.

Longer-Term Strategies

Your toolkit should also include practices that build your overall resilience and stress management capacity over time. Regular exercise combined with adequate sleep, along with healthy eating and mindfulness practices, enables you to stay calm and think clearly when facing pressure.

Environmental Supports

Assess your surroundings to determine whether they boost or reduce your stress levels. Better stress management occurs when you create structured peaceful study environments while following daily patterns and maintaining relationships with supportive individuals.

Professional Resources

The decision to seek help from teachers, counselors, parents, and other trusted adults demonstrates wisdom rather than weakness. These professionals offer additional stress management tools along with strategies and emotional regulation skill development support.

Chapter Summary

The transformation of Kevin *from test anxiety paralysis to developing effective stress management skills* demonstrates the direct relationship between emotional control and clear mental processing. Simple breathing exercises help us regain access to our thinking abilities by neutralizing the negative effects stress response activates in the brain. Learning physical relaxation techniques along with mental coping methods and environmental organizing skills enables people to develop their complete stress management abilities. We know that the mastery of stress management techniques produces benefits across every life domain because it enables people to handle difficult situations through intentional action instead of automatic responses.

Chapter 11: Drawing Your Ideas: The Magic of Mind Maps

Sophie Discovers Her Thinking Web

Sophie stared at her science book, feeling overwhelmed again. Tomorrow she had to make a presentation about rainforests, but there was so much information! The trees, animals, weather conditions, local residents, and issues confronting the rainforest made her head feel jumpy just thinking about it all.

"I can't remember everything!" she groaned to her older brother, Marcus, who was doing homework at the kitchen table. But Sophie didn't have to because she was about to discover something wonderful that would help her understand and remember how everything was connected.

Marcus looked up from his laptop. *"What if I showed you how to draw your thoughts? It's called a mind map, and it's like creating a picture of everything in your brain."*

"Draw my thoughts?" Sophie was curious now.

Marcus grabbed a blank piece of paper and drew a small circle in the center. *"This is your main idea,"* he said, writing "RAINFOREST" inside the circle. *"Now, what are the big things you learned about rainforests?"*

"Um... animals that live there, and the trees, and... oh! The weather?"

"Perfect!" Marcus drew three lines coming out from the center circle, like the spokes of a wheel. At the end of each line, he drew smaller circles and wrote "ANIMALS," "TREES," and "WEATHER."

Sophie's eyes lit up. *"It looks like a spiderweb!"*

"Exactly! And just like a spiderweb, it connects different points; your mind map connects different ideas. Now, what animals did you learn about?"

Sophie thought for a moment. *"Monkeys, colorful birds called parrots, and those big cats... jaguars!"*

Marcus drew three more lines coming from the "ANIMALS" circle and added these animals. Each idea branched out to connect more specific ideas, and she realized it was just like her mind making connections, but here she could see them.

As they continued, Sophie added information about tall trees, daily rain showers, and indigenous people. Soon the paper was filled with a colorful web of connected ideas.

"Wow," Sophie said, looking at their creation. *"I can see how everything in the rainforest works together! The trees need rain, the animals need trees, and the people protect the forest."*

The "magic" of mind maps is that you can see the big picture and remember details at the same time. And it makes studying fun because you are drawing instead of reading.

Key Lessons:

- Mind maps help organize lots of information by showing how ideas connect

- Drawing helps your brain remember better than just reading

- You can see both big ideas and small details at the same time

- Making connections between ideas helps you understand subjects better

How Mind Maps Help You Learn Better

Think of your brain like an enormous library. When you read a regular book or take notes in lines, it's like putting all the books on one long shelf, hard to find what you need! But a mind map is *like organizing your library by creating different rooms* and placing signs that point in various directions. You can quickly find what you're looking for and see how different books relate to each other.

Science: Create mind maps *about the solar system* with the sun in the center, then branch out to planets, and from each planet, add facts like size, temperature, and moons. You'll see how everything in space is connected!

History: Put a historical event in the center *(like the American Revolution)*, then branch out to causes, important people, major battles, and results. You'll understand not just what happened, but why it happened and what came next.

Environment: Start with "*PROTECTING EARTH*" in the center, then branch out to recycling, saving water, protecting animals, and reducing pollution. Each branch can show specific actions you can take.

Free Mind Map Websites Where Kids Can Create Their Own

Here are some fantastic websites where you can make digital mind maps for free. *Ask a grown-up to help you get started:*

1. **Coggle (www.coggle.it)**

Super easy to use with colorful branches

Works great for school projects

You can add pictures to make it more fun

The free version lets you *make 3 private maps*

2. MindMeister (www.mindmeister.com)

Has a kid-friendly design

Lets you work on maps with friends or family

Includes fun icons and colors

The free version gives you *3 mind maps*

3. Canva (www.canva.com)

This resource offers mind-map templates *specifically designed for students.*

Easy drag-and-drop features

Lots of fun graphics and colors to choose from

The free version has everything most kids need

4. SimpleMind (www.simplemind.eu)

On computers and tablets

Very simple to learn—great for beginners

The free version works *perfectly for school projects*

Has both colorful and simple design options

5. Milanote (www.milanote.com)

Great for visual learners

You can add photos, drawings, and notes

Perfect for creative projects

The free version includes up to *100 notes/images*

Activity: "My Learning Adventure Map"

What You'll Need:

You can use a large piece of paper or one of the websites mentioned above.

Colored pencils or markers

Your imagination!

Steps:

- *Choose Your Topic:* Pick something you're learning about in school, perhaps dinosaurs, your state's history, or how plants grow.

- *Draw Your Center:* In the middle of your paper, draw a circle and write your main topic. Make it colorful and fun!

- *Add Your Main Branches*: Think of 3-5 big categories related to your topic. Draw lines out from the center like tree branches and add these categories.

- *Grow Your Branches*: For each main category, add smaller branches with specific facts, examples, or details.

- *Make Connections*: Use different colored lines to connect related ideas from different branches. This shows how things work together!

- *Add Pictures*: Draw small pictures or symbols next to your words. Your brain remembers pictures better than just words.

- *Share Your Map*: Show your mind map to family members or friends and use it to teach them what you learned!

Mind Map Success Stories

Emma's Weather Map: Emma was confused about different types of weather until she created a mind map. She put "WEATHER" in the center, then branched out to sunny, rainy, snowy, and stormy weather. Under each type, she added what causes it, what it looks like, and what people do during that weather. Now she's the class weather expert!

David's Presidents Project: David had to learn about five U.S. presidents. Instead of trying to memorize facts from a book, he made a mind map for each president with branches for childhood, achievements, challenges, and fun facts. His presentation was so good that other kids asked him to teach them the mind map technique!

Aria's Animal Kingdom: Aria loves animals but couldn't keep track of different animal groups. Her mind map started with "ANIMALS" in the center, then branched to mammals, birds, fish, reptiles, and insects. Under each group, she added examples and special characteristics. Now she can easily explain the difference between a mammal and a reptile!

Tips for Amazing Mind Maps

- *Use Colors Wisely*: Give each main branch its own color, then use lighter shades of that color for smaller branches. This helps your eye follow ideas easily.

- *Keep Words Short*: Use 1-3 words per idea, not long sentences. Your brain processes short phrases faster.

- *Add Drawings*: Even simple stick figures or basic shapes help your brain remember information better.

- *Start Big,* Then Get Specific: Begin with broad categories, then add more detailed information as you branch out.

- *Make It Personal*: Add your own thoughts, questions, or connections to make the mind map meaningful to you.

When Mind Maps Work Best
Mind maps are super helpful when you need to:
- Understand how different things connect to each other

- Remember lots of information for a test

- Plan a story or creative project

- Solve problems by seeing all the pieces

- Prepare presentations or reports

- Study subjects with many related parts

Remember, **there's no "wrong" way to make a mind map.** The best mind map is the one that makes sense to YOU and helps YOU learn better. Some kids like neat, organized maps, while others prefer wild, creative ones with lots of colors and drawings. The important thing is that it helps your amazing thinking brain organize and remember information!

Your mind map is like your personal learning superpower, so use it to *unlock the connections between ideas* and **become a learning detective** in any subject you explore!

Appendix

Introduction for Parents and Caregivers

The stories and lessons in this book become more engaging when families practice critical thinking activities during their daily routines. This appendix contains enjoyable activities that help children build their thinking abilities while also building stronger family relationships and creating *positive home learning* experiences. One thing we always want to work on is the home environment and how it contributes to our children's development.

Do you regularly think about critical thinking development in your children? This opportunity enables you to start essential conversations that will prepare your children to become better thinkers, investigators, critical thinkers, and successful individuals in their adult lives. The ability to question and analyze information effectively stands as the most valuable skill you can teach your child. So everything you do now is going to form a basis for your child to build on in the future and in their adult lives.

These activities are presented as enjoyable family activities instead of traditional educational content. Kids don't want their home to be like their school, and that's the reason these activities have been planned for joy with plenty of learning involved. The activities aim to establish natural settings that allow children to *develop questioning skills and analyze problems* while solving them and expressing their thoughts in *environments that support their curiosity and accept mistakes*. Remember, **there are no mistakes**, only things that we have to reconsider to increase our learning.

Children need to learn questioning skills as their first essential life lesson. The practice of questioning should always *stem from valid reasons*. Questioning is key. Encourage your children to question and to come to you when they are curious or undecided about anything. You should be one of the first resources for them.

Simple Exercises for Everyday Moments

The Daily Detective Challenge

What You Need: Just curiosity and 5-10 minutes

The game requires you to select *an everyday household object*, which becomes the subject of detective work between family members. The investigation should focus on any household item, including furniture pieces and rugs as well as pictures on the walls and decorative objects. The players should alternate between asking these questions:

• Have you ever spotted something new about this object that you had not seen before? Encourage them to really look at the item carefully.

• What materials do you believe this object consists of? What process do you think was used to create this object? Who might have made it and where?

• What questions would you ask the person who designed this? If you could speak to the designer, what would you want to ask them?

• What modification would you make to this object if you had the chance? Should there be some changes to this item, and what would they be?

The activity *enables children to observe better while developing their questioning skills* and creative thinking abilities through exploration of hidden stories within everyday objects. The activity will introduce your child to new interests while helping them discover a new appreciation for everyday things.

The Martinez family dedicated ten minutes to studying their kitchen timer, which led to a discussion about *time measurement and counting* and sound production and timer design for alerting people. Does anybody know about *the Pomodoro Effect*? Know what it is? The Pomodoro timer resembles a tomato and serves as a tool to divide study sessions into shorter blocks, which enhances our ability to keep information. Check if purchasing this timer would be useful.

The "What If" Bedtime Game

What You Need: Imagination and a bedtime routine

The game requires players to create "what if" stories which they will then explore together during bedtime:

• Animals possess the ability to speak with humans. Your pet, along with neighborhood animals, would share what they want to communicate with you if they could speak. The discussion serves as a starting point to explore how scientists study animal behavior to understand their experiences better. The new language research goes beyond our previous understanding. We already know that dolphins have a particular language that they use in their groups. And whales also have a song that identifies each of them. Yes, every whale has its own song.

• Pictorial communication would become the only method we could use to express ourselves during an entire day. How would we determine our breakfast selection? The activity serves as an entry point to learning *American Sign Language*, which you can add to your bedtime educational activities. Your child should learn the *deaf emergency signs*, which they can find online. Encourage them to perform a search for these signs.

Family Tip: The questions should remain cheerful and optimistic when you ask them before bedtime. *The most complicated "what if" scenarios should be discussed during daytime hours.* The child will develop new questions or ask more questions later at bedtime.

The Evidence Hunt

You need to have an event from your family history (a lost object or an unexplained mess).

The game requires players to transform everyday family mysteries. (Who left the milk out? The dog's toy somehow reached the rooftop.) The game becomes a detective investigation.

• What evidence can we find?

The group explores alternative explanations for the events. It's a game that presents a classic case of '*Who done it*?'

The group needs to develop methods to verify their proposed solutions. What methods could they use? Where would they go to look for information?

• What questions have we forgotten?

Children *learn to collect data* while examining various solutions and solving problems systematically *through real-life experiences*.

Maintain a playful atmosphere during this activity because it serves as *a learning experience instead of creating blame or conflict*. It's a fun activity that encourages detective work.

Critical Thinking Games for Car Rides and Dinner Tables

The Perspective Game

The game is suitable for *car trips, restaurant delays, and family dining time*.

The game requires participants to select a visible or imaginable scene, which they will explain from different angles.

The *cooks explain their dinner preparation process* to the group. How do the cooks decide what to make, what recipe to use, and how much difficulty did they experience when doing all of this? What were the cooks thinking all the time?

The *family pet experiences the morning routine* differently than humans do, according to your imagination. The walk with the dog ends, but their mental state remains unknown during that time. You can be sure they think about something. What was the pet thinking?

The rainstorm experience from a plant's perspective, a person without an umbrella, and a duck's viewpoint makes for an excellent activity. This is a good one.

The game helps children *develop empathy skills* while teaching them to think flexibly and create new ideas and understand how different people or animals experience the same events differently. Do we ever think about plants and how they might enjoy a rainstorm?

The Question Chain Game

The game works during any time when you *spend 10-15 minutes together*. Great because it only calls for small bits of time.

The game begins with a *subject your child finds interesting* before exchanging questions that expand on previous statements.

Parent: *"You enjoy watching (dolphins). What stands out to you as the most fascinating aspect of (dolphins)?"* You should replace the subject with what your child expressed interest in. The most beneficial choice would be to select a specific wild animal. The child will direct the conversation while the parent needs to maintain a following role.

Child: "*They can talk to each other underwater.*" Parent: "*How do you suppose they acquired this ability to communicate underwater?*"

Child: "*They might have trained like we practice speaking with each other.*"

Parent: "*What knowledge do baby dolphins require to learn from their parents?*"

The game helps *children develop their curiosity* while teaching them to ask questions, connect ideas, and maintain useful dialogue. The discussion about wild animals *introduces environmental awareness* because it shows how all living things, including humans, experience effects from their surroundings.

The Solution Brainstorm

Perfect for family *dinners, weekend conversations*

Participants *solve basic problems* that affect families before they start developing solutions with *no criticism of the ideas.*

- The group discusses methods of setting a plant watering schedule. Plants should have the ability to *alert people about their needs.* Do they?

- The group explores methods of creating less stressful morning routines. What's causing the stress?

- The group needs to develop solutions that will assist elderly neighbors who face difficulties with high-shelf access and lawn maintenance.

- The group now evaluates which ideas show the most potential and each explains their reasoning.

The activity helps children *develop creative problem-solving abilities* and learn to evaluate solutions while understanding that various answers exist for each challenge. The activity demonstrates how people in our community support one another through their actions. Your child develops critical thinking abilities while *learning social competencies* during this activity time.

Reading Adventures That Build Critical Thinking

Books That Invite Questions and Discussions

The book recommendations follow reading level categories, although children learn at their own pace. Select reading materials that match your child's interests and reading abilities while reading simpler books together when they start meaningful discussions. You'll need to visit either the library or the local bookstore to get these books. Your children will benefit from this activity, which serves as an excellent starting point for reading these books together.

Beginning Readers (Ages 5-7)

"The Important Book" by Margaret Wise Brown

The book shows readers how to identify essential aspects of everyday things and life experiences.

The discussion here focuses on which items you would include in your personal "important book" about your family or school or favorite animal. A blank notebook might be available during this discussion for children to *note down their thoughts.*

"A Dark, Dark Tale" by Ruth Brown

The story structure in this book helps readers predict events, while its unexpected ending proves that *our initial beliefs can be incorrect.*

"Fortunately" by Remy Charlip

The book shows readers *how different people view the same events* through fortunate or unfortunate perspectives. It helps children develop *stronger coping abilities.*

Developing Readers (Ages 6-9)

"The Z Was Zapped" by Chris Van Allsburg

The book presents one mystery per page, which readers must solve by using visual evidence and their imagination.

The discussion focuses on how you solved the mystery of each letter disappearance. Which elements in the story provided you with the most important information for solving the mystery?

"Tuesday" by David Wiesner

The *wordless picture book* lets readers create their own explanations about the unexplained occurrences in the story.

"The Great Kapok Tree" by Lynne Cherry

The story presents various *environmental perspectives* to readers who can then evaluate different viewpoints about these issues.

Confident Readers (Ages 8-11)

"Hatchet" by Gary Paulsen

The *survival tale* demonstrates how people can develop problem-solving abilities and learn from their errors while adapting to new situations.

Before Reading

Examine the book cover to create predictions about the upcoming narrative.

Start by sharing their existing knowledge about the subject matter and its environment.

Create several questions that *you believe the book will resolve* during your reading.

During Reading

Stop reading periodically to inquire about upcoming events and the motivations behind character decisions.

Observe the moments when your predictions about the story don't match the actual events.

The story contains elements that you can relate to your personal life experiences. Give some examples when appropriate. It's always better to include real-life things that you have gone through and that your child may benefit from knowing.

After Reading

Examine which *plot elements shocked* them and explain their reasons for surprise.

The story revealed how *each character grows* throughout its narrative sequence.

The *story would present a different narrative* if the author chose to tell it from a different character's point of view.

The story contains *unresolved questions* that you should identify.

Creating a Critical Thinking Family Culture

Family Meeting Detective Style

The process of turning family gatherings into collaborative problem-solving activities should begin with this approach.

1. The family *works together to solve problems* instead of receiving decisions from others.

2. The group *listens to each member explain their point of view* regarding the situation.

3. The group *creates solutions* without making any immediate assessments about their quality.

4. The group analyzes *the advantages and disadvantages* of each possible solution.

5. The family *tests new solutions* through experiments before evaluating their effectiveness.

The Family Question Board

The family establishes a designated area (bulletin board or notebook or jar) for *posting interesting questions* that members discover or create.

The weekly addition of questions to the board could include:

- *Why do we dream? Do dreams mean anything?*

- Do birds possess a natural ability to find their migration paths through the air?

- Why do some people like spicy food? Does it exist because people have different taste preferences, and how does that happen?

The family can use weekend time and dinner hours to examine questions that members have written. The main objective of this activity is to experience collective curiosity rather than to achieve specific solutions. It's group cohesion and collective working together to find solutions to problems or answers to issues that have come up.

Celebrating Thinking, Not Just Results

Notice and Praise:

- Your decision process was impressive because you asked three different questions before making a choice.

- Your ability to change your decision after obtaining new information demonstrates excellent thinking skills. Applaud their thinking skills.

- Your consideration of how your decision would affect your sister shows genuine thoughtfulness. This is very important for kids to learn.

- Your thoughtful pause before answering shows you possess wise thinking abilities. It's always think first before you act.

Create Family Stories:

The family can exchange times when members showed special thinking abilities.

The family can discuss instances where errors resulted in valuable learning experiences. Remember, everything is learning, not failures.

The family honors times when members changed their decisions through evidence-based reasoning. Facts first, decision next.

Model Your Own Thinking

Children need to witness your process of solving problems, your willingness to modify your decisions when you receive new information and your ability to recognize when you lack understanding. Your willingness to learn alongside your children creates a stronger impact than providing all the correct answers.

Make Mistakes Welcome

Establish a family environment that *treats mistakes as chances to learn* instead of viewing them as unsuccessful attempts. When someone makes an error, you ask, "*What can we learn from this?*" instead of dwelling on the mistakes.

Keep It Joyful

The process of critical thinking should bring excitement to students instead of creating a sense of obligation. When an activity fails to work or becomes unenjoyable, you need to use a different approach. The development of lifelong curiosity and thoughtfulness requires positive supportive environments, which lead to successful learning.

Your child will receive their most valuable present through *teaching them to ask smart questions and solve problems* with wisdom and curiosity.

Bibliography

Anderson, Lorin W., and David R. Krathwohl, eds. A Taxonomy for Learning, Teaching, and Assessing: A Revision of Bloom's Taxonomy of Educational Objectives. New York: Longman, 2001.

Aoun, Joseph E. Robot-Proof: Higher Education in the Age of Artificial Intelligence. Cambridge: MIT Press, 2017.

Arnsten, Amy F. T. "Stress Signalling Pathways That Impair Prefrontal Cortex Structure and Function." Nature Reviews Neuroscience 10, no. 6 (2009): 410-422.

Baron, Jonathan. Thinking and Deciding. 4th ed. New York: Cambridge University Press, 2008.

Bazerman, Max H., and Don A. Moore. Judgment in Managerial Decision Making. 8th ed. Hoboken: John Wiley & Sons, 2013.

Beach, Lee Roy, and Terry Connolly. The Psychology of Decision Making: People in Organizations. 2nd ed. Thousand Oaks: Sage Publications, 2005.

Beck, Aaron T., and Brad A. Alford. Depression: Causes and Treatment. 2nd ed. Philadelphia: University of Pennsylvania Press, 2009.

Boice, Robert. Advice for New Faculty Members: Nihil Nimus. Boston: Allyn and Bacon, 2000.

Botti, Simona, and Sheena S. Iyengar. "The Dark Side of Choice: When Choice Impairs Social Welfare." Journal of Public Policy & Marketing 25, no. 1 (2006): 24-38.

Breakstone, Joel, Mark Smith, Sam Wineburg, Amie Rapaport, Jill Carle, Marshall Garland, and Anna Saavedra. "Students' Civic Online Reasoning: A National Portrait." Stanford Digital Repository, 2019.

Brown, Peter C., Henry L. Roediger III, and Mark A. McDaniel. Make It Stick: The Science of Successful Learning. Cambridge: Harvard University Press, 2014.

Chi, Michelene T. H., Miriam Bassok, Matthew W. Lewis, Peter Reimann, and Robert Glaser. "Self-Explanations: How Students Study and Use Examples in Learning to Solve Problems." Cognitive Science 13, no. 2 (1989): 145-182.

Clark, Andy, and David Chalmers. "The Extended Mind." Analysis 58, no. 1 (1998): 7-19.

Clark, Richard C., and Richard E. Mayer. E-Learning and the Science of Instruction. 4th ed. Hoboken: John Wiley & Sons, 2016.

Clear, James. Atomic Habits: An Easy & Proven Way to Build Good Habits & Break Bad Ones. New York: Avery, 2018.

Csikszentmihalyi, Mihaly. Creativity: Flow and the Psychology of Discovery and Invention. New York: Harper Collins, 1996.

Davidson, Richard J., and Bruce S. McEwen. "Social Influences on Neuroplasticity: Stress and Interventions to Promote Well-Being." Nature Neuroscience 15, no. 5 (2012): 689-695.

Davis, Mark H. "Measuring Individual Differences in Empathy: Evidence for a Multidimensional Approach." Journal of Personality and Social Psychology 44, no. 1 (1983): 113-126.

Dede, Chris, and John Richards, eds. Digital Teaching Platforms. New York: Teachers College Press, 2012.

Duckworth, Angela. Grit: The Power of Passion and Perseverance. New York: Scribner, 2016.

Duhigg, Charles. The Power of Habit: Why We Do What We Do in Life and Business. New York: Random House, 2012.

Durlak, Joseph A., Roger P. Weissberg, Allison B. Dymnicki, Rebecca D. Taylor, and Kriston B. Schellinger. "The Impact of Enhancing Students' Social and Emotional Learning: A Meta-Analysis of School-Based Universal Interventions." Child Development 82, no. 1 (2011): 405-432.

Eppler, Martin J., and Jeanne Mengis. "The Concept of Information Overload: A Review of Literature from Organization Science, Accounting, Marketing, MIS, and Related Disciplines." The Information Society 20, no. 5 (2004): 325-344.

Festinger, Leon. A Theory of Cognitive Dissonance. Stanford: Stanford University Press, 1957.

Flavell, John H. "Metacognition and Cognitive Monitoring: A New Area of Cognitive-Developmental Inquiry." American Psychologist 34, no. 10 (1979): 906-911.

Fogg, BJ. Tiny Habits: The Small Changes That Change Everything. Boston: Houghton Mifflin Harcourt, 2019.

Gilovich, Thomas. How We Know What Isn't So: The Fallibility of Human Reason in Everyday Life. New York: Free Press, 1991.

Guilford, J. P. "Creativity." American Psychologist 5, no. 9 (1950): 444-454.

Halpern, Diane F. Thought and Knowledge: An Introduction to Critical Thinking. 5th ed. New York: Psychology Press, 2014.

Heath, Chip, and Dan Heath. Decisive: How to Make Better Choices in Life and Work. New York: Crown Business, 2013.

Heath, Chip, and Dan Heath. Made to Stick: Why Some Ideas Survive and Others Die. New York: Random House, 2007.

Holstein, Kenneth, Bruce M. McLaren, and Vincent Aleven. "Student Learning Benefits of a Mixed-Reality Teacher Awareness Tool in AI-Enhanced Classrooms." Artificial Intelligence in Education 10947 (2018): 154-168.

Iyengar, Sheena, and Mark Lepper. "When Choice is Demotivating: Can One Desire Too Much of a Good Thing?" Journal of Personality and Social Psychology 79, no. 6 (2000): 995-1006.

Kahneman, Daniel. Thinking, Fast and Slow. New York: Farrar, Straus and Giroux, 2011.

Kahneman, Daniel, and Amos Tversky. "Prospect Theory: An Analysis of Decision under Risk." Econometrica 47, no. 2 (1979): 263-291.

Klayman, Joshua, and Young-Won Ha. "Confirmation, Disconfirmation, and Information in Hypothesis Testing." Psychological Review 94, no. 2 (1987): 211-228.

Kozyreva, Anastasia, Stephan Lewandowsky, and Ralph Hertwig. "Citizens Versus the Internet: Confronting Digital Challenges with Cognitive Tools." Psychological Science in the Public Interest 21, no. 3 (2020): 103-156.

Larrick, Richard P. "Debiasing." In Blackwell Handbook of Judgment and Decision Making, edited by Derek J. Koehler and Nigel Harvey, 316-338. Oxford: Blackwell Publishing, 2004.

Lewandowsky, Stephan, Ullrich K. H. Ecker, Colleen M. Seifert, Norbert Schwarz, and John Cook. "Misinformation and Its Correction: Continued Influence and Successful Debiasing." Psychological Science in the Public Interest 13, no. 3 (2012): 106-131.

Luckin, Rose. Machine Learning and Human Intelligence: The Future of Education for the 21st Century. London: UCL Institute of Education Press, 2018.

Lupien, Sonia J., Bruce S. McEwen, Megan R. Gunnar, and Christine Heim. "Effects of Stress Throughout the Lifespan on the Brain, Behaviour and Cognition." Nature Reviews Neuroscience 10, no. 6 (2009): 434-445.

Ma, Xiao, Zi-Qi Yue, Zhu-Qing Gong, Hong Zhang, Nai-Yue Duan, Yu-Tong Shi, Gao-Xia Wei, and You-Fa Li. "The Effect of Diaphragmatic Breathing on Attention, Negative Affect and Stress in Healthy Adults." Frontiers in Psychology 8 (2017): 874.

Mayer, Richard E. Multimedia Learning. 2nd ed. New York: Cambridge University Press, 2009.

Metzger, Miriam J. "Making Sense of Credibility on the Web: Models for Evaluating Online Information and Recommendations for Future Research." Journal of the American Society for Information Science and Technology 58, no. 13 (2007): 2078-2091.

Nickerson, Raymond S. "Confirmation Bias: A Ubiquitous Phenomenon in Many Guises." Review of General Psychology 2, no. 2 (1998): 175-220.

Papert, Seymour. Mindstorms: Children, Computers, and Powerful Ideas. 2nd ed. New York: Basic Books, 1993.

Payne, John W., James R. Bettman, and Eric J. Johnson. The Adaptive Decision Maker. Cambridge: Cambridge University Press, 1993.

Petty, Richard E., and John T. Cacioppo. Communication and Persuasion: Central and Peripheral Routes to Attitude Change. New York: Springer-Verlag, 1986.

Porges, Stephen W. "The Polyvagal Theory: New Insights into Adaptive Reactions of the Autonomic Nervous System." Cleveland Clinic Journal of Medicine 76, no. 4 (2009): S86-S90.

Reich, Justin, and Mehran Sahami. "The Power and Peril of AI in Education." Communications of the ACM 65, no. 2 (2022): 26-28.

Reivich, Karen, and Andrew Shatte. The Resilience Factor: 7 Keys to Finding Your Inner Strength and Overcoming Life's Hurdles. New York: Broadway Books, 2002.

Reutskaja, Elena, and Robin M. Hogarth. "Satisfaction in Choice as a Function of the Number of Alternatives: When 'Goods Satiate.'" Psychology & Marketing 26, no. 3 (2009): 197-203.

Rosenshine, Barak, Carla Meister, and Saul Chapman. "Teaching Students to Generate Questions: A Review of the Intervention Studies." Review of Educational Research 66, no. 2 (1996): 181-221.

Russo, J. Edward, and Paul J. H. Schoemaker. Decision Traps: Ten Barriers to Brilliant Decision-Making and How to Overcome Them. New York: Doubleday, 1989.

Sapolsky, Robert M. Why Zebras Don't Get Ulcers. 3rd ed. New York: Times Books, 2004.

Scheibehenne, Benjamin, Rainer Greifeneder, and Peter M. Todd. "Can There Ever Be Too Many Options? A Meta-Analytic Review of Choice Overload." Journal of Consumer Research 37, no. 3 (2010): 409-425.

Schraw, Gregory, Kent J. Crippen, and Kendall Hartley. "Promoting Self-Regulation in Science Education: Metacognition as Part of a Broader Perspective on Learning." Research in Science Education 36, no. 1-2 (2006): 111-139.

Schwartz, Barry. The Paradox of Choice: Why More Is Less. New York: Ecco, 2004.

Seligman, Martin E. P. Learned Optimism: How to Change Your Mind and Your Life. New York: Vintage Books, 2006.

Simon, Herbert A. "Rational Choice and the Structure of the Environment." Psychological Review 63, no. 2 (1956): 129-138.

Smith, Stacy M., Leandre R. Fabrigar, and Meghan E. Powell. "The Role of Information-Processing Capacity and Goals in Attitude-Congruent Selective Exposure Effects." Personality and Social Psychology Bulletin 34, no. 7 (2008): 948-964.

Stanovich, Keith E. What Intelligence Tests Miss: The Psychology of Rational Thought. New Haven: Yale University Press, 2009.

Sweller, John. "Cognitive Load Theory, Learning Difficulty, and Instructional Design." Learning and Instruction 4, no. 4 (1994): 295-312.

Torrance, E. Paul. Torrance Tests of Creative Thinking. Bensenville: Scholastic Testing Service, 1974.

Vygotsky, Lev S. Mind in Society: The Development of Higher Psychological Processes. Cambridge: Harvard University Press, 1978.

Ward, Andrew, and Barry Schwartz. "Doing Better but Feeling Worse: The Paradox of Choice." In Positive Psychology in Practice, edited by P. Alex Linley and Stephen Joseph, 86-104. Hoboken: John Wiley & Sons, 2004.

Wason, Peter C. "On the Failure to Eliminate Hypotheses in a Conceptual Task." Quarterly Journal of Experimental Psychology 12, no. 3 (1960): 129-140.

Willingham, Daniel T. Why Don't Students Like School? A Cognitive Scientist Answers Questions About How the Mind Works and What It Means for the Classroom. San Francisco: Jossey-Bass, 2009.

Wineburg, Sam, and Sarah McGrew. "Lateral Reading: Reading Less and Learning More When Evaluating Digital Information." Stanford History Education Group Working Paper No. 2017-A1, 2017.

Yates, J. Frank. Judgment and Decision Making. Englewood Cliffs: Prentice Hall, 1990.

Zeidner, Moshe. Test Anxiety: The State of the Art. New York: Plenum Press, 1998.

Zimmerman, Barry J. "Becoming a Self-Regulated Learner: An Overview." Theory Into Practice 41, no. 2 (2002): 64-70.

About the Author

D r. Patricia A. Farrell is a licensed psychologist, published author of multiple self-help books and videos, former WebMD psychologist expert/consultant, medical consultant for Social Security Disability Determinations, Alzheimer's psychiatric researcher at Mt. Sinai Medical Center (NYC), and an educator who has taught at the college, graduate, and postgraduate levels.

Her influence extends to the pharmaceutical and marketing industries, where she serves as a consultant and has appeared on major TV news programs in the US and abroad. In addition, Dr. Farrell provides continuing education modules for mental healthcare professionals and has contributed to USMLE medical school prep courses. She shares her knowledge through her YouTube channel and her daily contributions to **Bluesky** (@carpenter22,bsky.social) and Medium. com articles. Dr. Farrell's achievements are recognized in *Who's Who in the World, Who's Who in America,* and *Who's Who in American Women.*

A member of the American Psychological Association and the SAG-AFTRA union, Dr. Farrell is a former board member of the NJ Board of Psychological Examiners, a former psychiatry preceptor at UMDNJ, and a former board of directors member of Bergen Pines Hospital (now Bergen Regional Hospital).

Books by Patricia A. Farrell, Ph.D.

How to Be Your Own Therapist

When You Can't Pour From an Empty Glass: CBT Skills for Exhausted Caregivers

The Little Book on Learning Big Critical Thinking Skills

It's Not All in Your Head: Anxiety, Depression, Mood Swings and Multiple Sclerosis

Unfiltered: Beneath the noise of our thoughts lies the true narrative of our minds

Unfiltered Again: A behind-the-scenes look at healthcare, medicine and mental health

When You Can't Pour From an Empty Glass: CBT Skills for Exhausted Caregivers

A Social Security Disability Psychological Claims Handbook: A simple guide to understanding your SSD claim for psychological impairments and unraveling the maze of decision-making

A Social Security Disability Psychological Claims Guidebook for Children's Benefits

The Disability Accessible US Parks in All 50 States: A Comprehensive Guide

Birding in the US NOW!: A birding guide for individuals with disabilities

A Special Request

If this book has touched your heart, sparked your curiosity, or simply entertained you along the way, I'd be incredibly grateful if you could take a moment to share your thoughts with a review on Amazon or wherever you discovered this book. Your words not only help other readers find books they'll love, but they also mean the world to authors like me who pour their hearts into every page. Thank you for being part of this journey, and for helping stories find their way to the readers who need them most.

www.ingramcontent.com/pod-product-compliance
Lightning Source LLC
Chambersburg PA
CBHW021110090426
42738CB00006B/578